THE OFFICIAL COOKBOOK

THE OFFICIAL COOKBOOK

From Aaaay to Zucchini Bread

CHRISTINA WARD

INSIGHT
EDITIONS

SAN RAFAEL · LOS ANGELES · LONDON

Contents

Introduction

Sunday, Monday, *Happy Days*! Tuesday, Wednesday, *Happy Days*! Admit it, you're humming along. And now you're thinking of the Cunningham's kitchen and Arnold's Drive-In where all are welcome to grab a snack and hang out with friends. Welcome to *Happy Days: The Official Cookbook: From Aaaay to Zucchini Bread*—a cookbook that pays homage to the beloved television show that captured the hearts of millions. Step back into the nostalgia of the 1950s and 1960s with a collection of recipes inspired by the iconic characters, memorable moments, and the nostalgic era of *Happy Days*. Whether you're a fan of Richie, Fonzie, or Mrs. C., get ready to embark on a culinary journey that celebrates the spirit of this classic TV series.

Within these pages, you'll discover recipes that reflect the flavors and charm of the time. From classic American comfort food to retro diner delights, each dish is designed to transport you to the cozy booths of Arnold's and the Cunninghams' dining room. Get ready to recreate the flavors that made *Happy Days* such a joyful and unforgettable experience.

In addition to delectable recipes, there are trivia questions about the show, the characters, the actors, and the history of *Happy Days*. Test yourself and your family while dinner is cooking! If you're like Fonzie and hate waiting, then we've got you covered. A handy trivia answer key is included at the back of the book. But we think you'll get a perfectamundo score without it.

So, dust off your apron, put on a copy of *Fonzie Favorites*, and hop into the kitchen as we cook up a storm of flavors. Whether you're planning a date night at Chez Antoine, hosting a rockin' sock hop party, indulging in weekend comfort food, or looking to relive the magic of *Happy Days*, this cookbook is your recipe to a culinary journey filled with warmth, laughter, and delicious old-fashioned fun.

With easy-to-follow instructions and ingredients, *Happy Days: The Official Cookbook* is designed for both experienced cooks and kitchen novices alike. Each recipe captures the essence of the show while incorporating modern techniques and flavors to suit modern tastes.

Now let's turn back the clock and celebrate friendship, family, and good food as we embark on a culinary adventure that will leave you saying, "Aaaay! These recipes are cool, just like The Fonz!" Get ready to rock and roll in the kitchen as you bring the flavors of *Happy Days* into your home.

Happy cooking!

Breakfast

Breakfast is the most important meal of the day, but it was often the opening scene for many episodes of *Happy Days*. We'd see Marion bustling to get lunches prepared and breakfast made so she could get her busy family off to work and school. Oh, and of course, there was always a brown bag for Fonzie. Early episodes heard Mrs. C. often exclaim, *"Children, you're not eating!"* So, don't waste a morsel and start the day with breakfast lovingly prepared by the one and only Mrs. Marion Cunningham, housewife extraordinaire and "mom" to the entire gang.

"Dude Ranch" Breakfast Skillet

Season six saw the entire gang undertake a big adventure as they traveled to Colorado to save the Bar-A Dude Ranch owned by Marion's Uncle Ben. Fonzie finds out that he may not be the coolest dude on the ranch when Richie attracts the attention of a beautiful wrangler. Will Fonzie find his Aaaay again? Al takes over the chuckwagon to serve tasty vittles to the hungry temporary ranch hands. What is Al going to do with that giant side of beef? Stay tuned!

PREP TIME: *20 minutes* | **COOK TIME:** *20 minutes* | **YIELD:** *4 to 6 servings or 1 very hungry buckaroo!* | **DIETARY NOTE:** *Gluten-Free*

6 slices bacon, chopped

1 small onion, diced

1 medium red bell pepper, diced

1 medium green bell pepper, diced

4 to 6 small Yukon Gold potatoes, diced (about 2 pounds)

6 eggs

Salt and ground black pepper, to taste

1 cup shredded cheddar cheese

Fresh parsley, chopped for garnish (optional)

In a large skillet, cook the chopped bacon over medium heat until crispy. Remove the bacon from the skillet, leaving the bacon drippings in the pan.

Add the diced onion, red bell pepper, green bell pepper, and diced potatoes to the skillet. Cook over medium heat, stirring occasionally, until the potatoes are golden brown and cooked through, about 10 to 12 minutes.

While the potatoes are cooking, in a separate bowl, whisk the eggs with a pinch of salt and pepper.

Once the potatoes are browned, push the potatoes and vegetables to one side of the skillet, creating a space for the eggs. Pour the whisked eggs into the cleared space.

Allow the eggs to cook undisturbed for a minute or two until they begin to set around the edges. Then, gently scramble the eggs with a spatula, incorporating them with the potatoes and vegetables.

Sprinkle the cooked bacon pieces evenly over the mixture.

Continue to cook for about 5 minutes, stirring occasionally, until the eggs are fully scrambled to your desired consistency.

Sprinkle the shredded cheddar cheese over the top of the skillet mixture. Cover the skillet with a lid or foil and let it sit for a few minutes until the cheese melts.

Remove the lid and give the skillet breakfast a final stir to evenly distribute the melted cheese.

Serve the "Dude Ranch" Breakfast Skillet hot, garnished with fresh chopped parsley if desired.

═══ NOTE ═══

Customize this recipe by adding additional ingredients such as diced ham, mushrooms, or spinach. You can also serve the skillet breakfast with a side of toast, tortillas, or salsa for added flavor.

Trivia

On the ranch, we discover that Marion has a special talent. What is it?

Blueberry Hill Pancakes

You might find a thrill on Blueberry Hill (which must be close to Inspiration Point). But what if the thrill is gone? Console yourself with Richie's favorite breakfast of Blueberry Hill Pancakes until your "Sugar Lips" arrives. Yowsa!

PREP TIME: *15 minutes* | **COOK TIME:** *3 to 5 minutes per batch* | **YIELD:** *about twelve 6-inch hotcakes* | **DIETARY NOTE:** *Vegetarian*

3 cups all-purpose flour

1 tablespoon sugar

1 teaspoon salt

1½ teaspoons baking powder

1½ teaspoons baking soda

1 cup buckwheat flour

1¼ cup buttermilk

4 eggs, beaten

½ cup vegetable oil

1 cup dried blueberries

Neutral (unflavored) nonstick pan spray or 2 teaspoons butter

Into a medium-sized bowl, sift together the all-purpose flour, sugar, salt, baking powder, and baking soda. Stir in buckwheat flour.

In a separate bowl, combine buttermilk and eggs and stir until blended. Add buttermilk-egg mixture to dry mixture. Add vegetable oil. Stir until lightly blended. Add in dried blueberries and gently fold into batter. (Small lumps in the batter are okay; don't over-stir.)

Over medium-high heat, warm griddle pan and lightly coat with nonstick baking spray or 2 teaspoons of butter. Carefully pour or ladle ½ cup of pancake batter onto griddle. Cook approximately 3 to 5 minutes until bubbles appear at edges, then flip pancake over. Cook another 3 to 5 minutes until pancake is browned. Cook longer for darker pancakes.

Top with a light sprinkle of powdered sugar, a dollop of blueberry jam and whipped cream, and a generous pour of 100% Wisconsin maple syrup.

NOTE

If making for a crowd, pancakes can be placed on a baking sheet and held in a warm oven until serving.

Trivia

Who made "Blueberry Hill" a hit song in 1956?

Joanie's French Toast

While Richie loves blueberry pancakes, Joanie loves her mom's French Toast! Marion wakes up early to make everyone's favorite after she accidentally crashes the DeSoto in Arnold's. Will French Toast stop the police from asking questions? No, but just like Mrs. Cunningham, make these early and keep them warm in the oven so breakfast isn't ruined . . . even if the car is.

PREP TIME: *15 minutes* | **COOK TIME:** *5 to 10 minutes per batch* | **YIELD:** *12 pieces* | **DIETARY NOTE:** *Vegetarian*

1 loaf thick-cut white sandwich bread

6 eggs

1 cup whole milk

1 teaspoon 100% pure vanilla extract

1 teaspoon cinnamon

¼ cup butter

Neutral (unflavored) nonstick pan spray

The day before making, remove bread from packaging, lay out on cooking sheet and place on top of stove to air dry the bread. Bread should be slightly stale when ready to use.

In a medium-sized bowl, crack open eggs. Add milk. Whisk together until frothy. Add in vanilla and cinnamon; whisk again. (The cinnamon may clump and not be thoroughly integrated; this is normal.)

Pour some of the egg mixture into a pie plate, approximately 1 inch full. Place one or two pieces of bread into the mixture and soak for 3 minutes. Turn the pieces over and soak for another 2 minutes.

While bread is soaking, spray griddle pan with nonstick spray and place on burner over medium-high heat. Add 1 tablespoon of butter and move around until pan is coated.

Carefully lift soaked bread with spatula flipper and place into pan. Cook approximately 3 minutes and flip over to cook another 5 to 10 minutes until toast reaches desired level of doneness. French toast should be golden brown and not scorched. If the first pieces are too dark, reduce heat to medium.

Hold cooked toast in warm oven as you refill pie plate with mixture and repeat soaking and cooking steps.

Serve on a warmed plate with fresh fruit when all pieces are cooked. Top with any of these items: maple syrup, powdered sugar (½ teaspoon, sifted), dollop of marmalade or favorite jam, whipped cream.

Cunningham's Strengthening Scottish Oatmeal

What happens when bullies threaten Richie Cunningham? Richie fights back! The twenty bucks borrowed from his dad buys jujitsu lessons from a mysterious teacher, but before he can practice, the training regimen requires body-building fuel like Strengthening Oatmeal!

PREP TIME: *5 minutes* | **COOK TIME:** *30 minutes* | **YIELD:** *4 to 6 servings* | **DIETARY NOTE:** *Vegetarian, Gluten-Free*

1 cup steel-cut oats (sometimes called Irish oats)

3 cups whole or 2% milk

½ teaspoon kosher or sea salt

1 teaspoon brown sugar (if making sweet)

Unsalted butter

Combine oats and milk in the saucepan. Bring oats and milk to simmer over medium-high heat for 10 minutes. Add salt and, if making sweet, brown sugar.

Reduce heat to medium and continue to simmer and cook uncovered for 20 minutes while stirring frequently but slowly, until porridge is thickened but not stiff. (If oats are too firm to your taste, stir in additional milk, ¼ cup at a time, and continue cooking until desired texture of oats is reached.)

Scoop oatmeal into warmed bowls and top with a pat of butter.

IF MAKING SWEET, YOU CAN:

Mix in ½ cup of chopped apples and ¼ cup of chopped walnuts.

Mix in ¼ cup of dried cherries and ¼ cup of sliced almonds.

Mix in ¼ cup of dried blueberries and ¼ cup of chopped pecans.

Mix in 1 tablespoon of peanut butter and 1 tablespoon of your choice of jelly.

Substitute brown sugar for 1 tablespoon of maple syrup and top with dollop of whipped cream.

Substitute brown sugar for 2 tablespoons of honey and top with ¼ cup honey-roasted peanuts.

IF MAKING SAVORY, YOU CAN:

Top with caramelized onions and mushrooms with a dash of black pepper.

Top with 1 ounce of shredded cheddar or Colby cheese.

Top with a pouched egg and a dash of black pepper.

Stir in 1 tablespoon 100% peanut butter (unsweetened) and dash of hot chile pepper oil.

Substitute water with chicken broth.

Trivia

Who was the mysterious jujitsu teacher Matsuo Takahashi?

Marion: *Good morning, Richie. Would you like corn flakes for breakfast, dear?*

Richie: *I never want corn flakes again. Oatmeal.*

Marion: *Well, I thought you liked corn fla—*

Richie: *[slaps the table] OATMEAL!!!!*

"Richie Fights Back," Season 3, Episode 6

"Morning, Mrs. C.!" Granola

If Richie ate this oaty, nut-filled granola along with his Cunningham's Strengthening Scottish Oatmeal (page 14), those bullies wouldn't have stood a chance.

PREP TIME: *15 minutes* | **COOK TIME:** *36 hours ferment and 6 hours dehydrate*
YIELD: *twelve ½-cup servings* | **DIETARY NOTE:** *Vegetarian, Gluten-Free*

1 heaping cup expeller-pressed coconut oil

10 cups rolled oats

1 cup full-fat unflavored yogurt

1½ cups Grade B maple syrup

3 tablespoons cinnamon

½ tablespoon ground nutmeg

1 tablespoon 100% pure vanilla extract

1½ to 3 teaspoons kosher salt

1 cup halved pecans

2 cups dried cherries or cranberries

Place coconut oil into a microwave-safe bowl and heat until just melted. In a large bowl, add the oats, then gently but thoroughly coat the oats in the melted coconut oil. Then, add the yogurt and repeat thorough mixing. Cover well with plastic wrap or fitted lid and let stand at room temperature for 24 to 30 hours.

The next day, mix maple syrup, spices, vanilla, and salt in a small saucepan. Warm over very low heat until blended. Let cool.

Add maple-spice mixture to the oat mixture and blend thoroughly. Add in nuts and dried fruit and mix evenly.

Preheat oven to lowest temperature setting, usually about 250°F. Spread the mixture out on a parchment-lined baking sheet and gently press into pan evenly until about ½ inch thick.

Place baking sheet into the oven and bake for 6 hours. When completely cooled, break granola into smaller pieces and store in an air-tight container.

"Cunningham, with that Howdy Doody face you can only be so tough." —Fonzie

"Richie Fights Back," Season 3, Episode 6

Mr. C.'s Weekend Hash
with Poached Eggs

Like many 1950s dads, Howard Cunningham served his country during World War II. While he wasn't a decorated hero, he did his part as a standard-issue Army cook. So, when the weekend arrived, Mr. C. took over the kitchen to rustle up some mess for his troops with a delicious version of good ol' army hash.

PREP TIME: *15 minutes* | **COOK TIME:** *20 minutes* | **YIELD:** *2 to 4 servings* | **DIETARY NOTE:** *Gluten-Free*

2 tablespoons vegetable oil

1 onion, chopped

2 garlic cloves, minced

2 medium potatoes, peeled and diced (about 1 pound)

1 bell pepper, diced

2 cups leftover pot roast, shredded or diced

Salt and ground black pepper, to taste

1 teaspoon dried thyme

1 teaspoon dried rosemary

Chopped fresh parsley for garnish (optional)

Shredded cheese (optional)

Hot sauce (optional)

Fresh eggs (as many as desired)

Water

Pinch of salt, to taste

Pinch of ground black pepper, to taste

NOTE

This recipe is a great way to use up leftover Mr. C.'s Favorite Pot Roast (page 112), but if you don't have any leftover, you can also cook a fresh roast specifically for making the hash. Simply cook the roast until tender, shred or dice it, and proceed with the recipe as directed.

Heat the vegetable oil in a large skillet or frying pan over medium heat. Add the chopped onion and minced garlic to the pan and sauté until the onion becomes translucent and the garlic is fragrant. Add the diced potatoes to the pan and cook until they start to brown and become crispy on the outside. Stir occasionally to prevent sticking.

Stir in the diced bell pepper and continue cooking for a few more minutes until the bell pepper is slightly softened. Add the shredded or diced pot roast to the pan and mix well with the vegetables. Season the hash with salt, pepper, dried thyme, and dried rosemary. Adjust the seasonings to your taste.

Cook the hash mixture for a few more minutes until everything is heated through. Remove from heat and serve the pot roast hash hot. Optionally, you can top the hash with some fresh chopped parsley, shredded cheese, or a drizzle of hot sauce for added flavor.

Fill a large, shallow saucepan with water, about 2 to 3 inches deep. Bring the water to a gentle simmer over medium heat.

Crack one egg into a small bowl or ramekin. (This will make it easier to slide the egg into the water later.) Use a spoon to create a gentle whirlpool in the simmering water. The swirling motion will help the egg whites wrap around the yolk nicely. Carefully slide the cracked egg into the center of the swirling water. The whirlpool motion will help the egg maintain a round shape as it cooks. The swirling water will also push the egg toward the side of the pan. If your egg remains in the center, gently push it to the side as you stir the water to keep the whirlpool moving. Repeat steps for each egg, ensuring there is enough space between them in the pan.

Allow the eggs to cook for about 3 to 4 minutes for a runny yolk or 5 to 6 minutes for a firmer yolk. Use a slotted spoon to carefully lift each poached egg out of the water, allowing any excess water to drain.

Place each poached egg on top of the plated serving of hash and add salt and pepper to taste.

Pork Sausage Apple Roulade Roast

Jenny Piccalo is the most boy-crazy teenager in Milwaukee . . . and she's teaching Joanie all her secrets. Is she a bad influence? Well, when you try to steal a park statue, what are the Cunningham's to think? Roscoe Piccalo's patience may be strained with Jenny and her equally boy-crazy sisters but he loves all his girls—including Mrs. Piccalo. Try this Piccalo family slumber party favorite that can be made ahead before the girls practice kissing on their pillows.

PREP TIME: *30 minutes* | **COOK TIME:** *60 minutes* | **YIELD:** *8 to 10 servings*

- ⅓ cup finely chopped white onion
- 2 cups finely chopped unpeeled and washed apples (mix of sweet and tart apples)
- 1 cup small, torn pieces baguette or other rustic bread
- 1 cup wheat germ
- 2 tablespoons brown sugar
- 2 pounds seasoned bulk pork breakfast sausage

Preheat the oven to 350°F.

Chop onions and apples into small pieces and place in bowl. Add bread pieces, wheat germ, and brown sugar. Mix until all ingredients are evenly distributed. Set aside.

Lay wax paper sheets on work surface, then spread and pat sausage into an 8-by-6-inch rectangle that is evenly ½ inch thick.

Take apple mixture and cover the sausage rectangle. Beginning on the shorter edge, carefully tuck and roll the edge toward the center of the rectangle. After about 6 inches, use wax paper to assist in keeping the roulade tight while you continue rolling. When you reach the end, use your hands to gently press the ends into an even edge.

Place parchment paper in baking dish. Carefully place roulade into pan. Bake uncovered for 60 minutes. Remove from the oven, and cover with aluminum foil tent to rest for 10 minutes.

Slice to serve.

NOTE

Can be prepared up to 24 hours in advance and stored in refrigerator before cooking.

Trivia

Jenny Piccalo was a regular character on the show. Who was the actress who played her? And who was the actor who played Roscoe Piccalo?

Salads

Mrs. Cunningham's short-lived job at Arnold's Drive-In saw her trying to get the gang to put down the French fries and eat something healthy. She always served vegetables at home—why shouldn't Arnold's offer salads like they serve at Chez Antoine?

Leopard Lodge Potato Salad

It's the Leopard Lodge picnic and Howard is making the Potato Salad . . . 100 pounds of potato salad! Not just any potato salad either—it's Howard's favorite, German style. He's the only person Marion knows who doesn't like mayonnaise. (Psst, Marion went ahead and made American potato salad, too. Turn the page for her recipe!)

Howard's German Style

PREP TIME: *20 minutes* | **COOK TIME:** *10 to 20 minutes* | **CHILL TIME:** *20 minutes* | **YIELD:** *10 to 12 servings*

4 slices cooked bacon, minced

4 cups ¼ inch sliced red potatoes (skin on)

1½ cups minced white onion

2 tablespoons all-purpose flour

1½ teaspoons kosher salt

Dash of ground black pepper

3 tablespoons apple cider vinegar

1 cup water

In a large skillet, cook the minced bacon over medium heat until crispy. Remove the bacon from the skillet and set aside to cool, leaving the bacon drippings in the pan.

In a small stock pot, add 2 quarts of water and bring to boil over high heat. While water is boiling, wash potatoes then cut into ¼-inch-thick slices. Add potato slices to boiling water. Cook about 10 to 15 minutes until potatoes are soft, yet still holding their shape.

Remove potatoes from heat, drain, and rinse with cool water. Set aside.

In the same skillet that you used to cook the bacon, add onions and cook over medium heat until onions are soft and translucent. Sprinkle the flour over the onions and stir to coat them evenly. Cook for about 1 minute. Add salt and pepper. Slowly add the vinegar and water to the skillet mixture, stirring continuously to avoid lumps. Cook for 2 to 3 minutes until thickened. Remove from heat.

Place the sliced potatoes into a large bowl and pour the warm dressing over them. Gently toss to coat the potatoes.

Add the cooled bacon to the potato mixture and gently fold it in. Season with salt and pepper to taste. Let the potato salad rest for at least 20 minutes to allow the flavors to meld together.

Trivia

The Cunningham's neighbor, Mr. Wilson, only appeared once but was portrayed by someone very familiar to the *Happy Days* cast and crew. Who was it?

Marion's American Style

PREP TIME: *20 minutes* | **COOK TIME:** *10 to 20 minutes* | **CHILL TIME:** *60 minutes*
YIELD: *10 to 12 servingss* | **DIETARY NOTE:** *Vegetarian, Gluten-Free*

6 to 7 cups Russet potatoes, peeled and cubed (about 3 pounds)

1 tablespoon white vinegar

4 large eggs

1 cup mayonnaise

2 tablespoons stone-ground mustard

6 tablespoons white wine vinegar

½ cup finely chopped celery (about 3 ribs)

½ cup finely chopped red onion

2 tablespoons pickle relish (sweet or dill, cook's choice—can substitute with chopped pickles)

1 tablespoon sugar (optional)

Pinch of salt, to taste

Pinch of ground black pepper, to taste

Paprika, for garnish (optional)

Chopped fresh parsley, for garnish (optional)

Place the cubed potatoes in a large pot and cover with cold water. Add a pinch of salt and the white vinegar to the water. Bring the water to a boil over medium-high heat and cook the potatoes until they are tender but still firm, about 10 to 15 minutes.

While the potatoes are cooking, place the eggs in a separate saucepan and cover them with cold water. Bring the water to a boil over medium-high heat. Once the water reaches a boil, reduce the heat slightly and let the eggs simmer for about 10 minutes.

Remove the eggs from the hot water and transfer them to a bowl of ice water to cool. Let them sit for a few minutes, then peel and chop the eggs into small pieces.

Drain the cooked potatoes and let them cool completely in a colander.

In a large mixing bowl, add the mayonnaise, mustard, white wine vinegar, chopped celery, red onion, and pickle relish. If you prefer a sweeter potato salad, add the optional sugar. Mix well to combine.

Add the cooled potatoes and chopped eggs to the dressing mixture. Gently fold everything together until the potatoes and eggs are evenly coated. Season the potato salad with salt and pepper to taste. Adjust the seasoning according to your preference.

Cover the bowl with plastic wrap and refrigerate for at least 1 hour to allow the flavors to meld together. Before serving, give the potato salad a gentle stir. Garnish it with a sprinkle of paprika and chopped fresh parsley.

 PAIRS WELL with Arnold's Drive-In Burgers (page 41), Arnold's Air-Fried Chicken Stand Tenders (page 135), and Hot Diggity Dog and Daddy-O Dog (page 43).

Cunningham Coleslaw

Al Delvecchio may have been the guy behind the fryer, but he knew that a crisp and creamy coleslaw was the best alternative to fries and onion rings on a hot summer day at Marion's Uncle's Colorado dude ranch. While the gang gets ready for the big rodeo, Al prepares a feast that includes the Cunningham Coleslaw to satisfy all the hungry dudes and dudettes.

PREP TIME: *20 minutes* | **COOK TIME:** *20 minutes* | **YIELD:** *4 to 6 servings* | **DIETARY NOTE:** *Vegetarian, Gluten-Free*

1 small head cabbage, finely shredded (about 2 pounds)

2 large carrots, peeled and grated (about 1 pound)

1 small white onion, thinly sliced (about a half pound)

½ to 1 cup mayonnaise (full amount for extra-creamy coleslaw)

2 tablespoons apple cider vinegar

1 tablespoon granulated sugar

1 teaspoon prepared Dijon mustard

Salt and ground black pepper, to taste

½ teaspoon garlic powder

In a large mixing bowl, combine the cabbage, onions, and carrots.

In a separate small bowl, whisk together the mayonnaise, apple cider vinegar, granulated sugar, Dijon mustard, salt, and pepper until well combined.

Pour the dressing over the cabbage, onion, and carrot mixture in the large bowl. Toss well to coat all the ingredients evenly with the dressing.

Taste the coleslaw and adjust the seasoning if needed by adding more salt, pepper, or garlic powder to taste.

Allow the coleslaw to chill in the refrigerator for at least 30 minutes to an hour before serving. This allows the flavors to meld together and for the cabbage to slightly soften.

Toss the coleslaw before serving.

Serve the traditional coleslaw as a classic side dish to accompany Arnold's Drive-In Burgers (page 41), Hot Diggity Dog and Daddy-O Dog (page 43), and Slow-Roasted Brisket (page 109).

Trivia

The second of the three "Westward Ho!" episodes features an original song titled "Rodeo Cowboy." Who wrote and sang the song?

Wedge Salad

Chez Antoine was *thee* place to celebrate anniversaries and impress a date. The ambience, the wine, and of course, the food, would set the mood for finding a few thrills. Richie took his best girl to Chez Antoine. Joanie's date was spoiled by Chachi there. Fonzie took Ashley and Heather. And Howard and Marion always celebrated their wedding anniversary with a multi-course feast starting with a simple, fresh, and delicious wedge salad. Who would have thought a salad could make you feel frisky?!

PREP TIME: *15 minutes* | **COOK TIME:** *15 minutes* | **YIELD:** *one head of lettuce yields 4 servings* | **DIETARY NOTE:** *Gluten-Free*

1 head iceberg lettuce

¼ cup ranch dressing

4 to 6 strips cooked bacon, crumbled

½ cup cherry tomatoes, halved

¼ cup red onion, thinly sliced

¼ cup blue cheese, crumbled

Salt and ground black pepper, to taste

Fresh chives, chopped, for garnish (optional)

Rinse the head of iceberg lettuce under cold water and pat it dry. Remove any outer wilted leaves. Cut the head of lettuce into quarters or wedges, making sure to keep the core intact to hold the wedge shape.

Place each lettuce wedge on a serving plate or platter.

Drizzle the ranch dressing over each wedge of lettuce, ensuring it covers the surface. Sprinkle the crumbled bacon, cherry tomatoes, red onion slices, and blue cheese evenly over each wedge. Season with a pinch of salt and black pepper to taste. Garnish with freshly chopped chives, if desired.

Serve Wedge Salad immediately.

 PAIRS WELL with Oven-Broasted Chicken (page 133), Sunday Baked Ham (page 120), and Chicken Cordon Bleu (page 140).

NOTE

Prepare bacon using preferred method. (Frying, baking, air fryer, or microwave are all acceptable.)

Trivia

We know him as Chachi Arcola. What's his given first name?

Pfister Salad

Who could have predicted that Fonzie would fall for sophisticated single mom Ashley Pfister? But when Fonzie takes Ashley and her daughter Heather to Chez Antoine, he's surprised by the menu. Frog legs? At least Fonzie doesn't have to pick his own frog. We'll stick with the Pfister Salad, Jacques!

PREP TIME: *20 minutes* | **COOK TIME:** *60 minutes* | **YIELD:** *4 to 6 servings* | **DIETARY NOTE:** *Vegetarian, Gluten-Free*

2 cups unpeeled, washed, chopped apples (1-inch chunks)

1 cup chopped celery

1 cup red seedless grapes, halved

½ cup chopped toasted walnuts

½ cup dried cranberries (can substitute with raisins or dried cherries)

½ cup plain Greek yogurt

¼ cup mayonnaise

1 tablespoon lemon juice

1 tablespoon honey

Pinch of kosher salt, to taste

Pinch of ground black pepper, to taste

1 head Bibb lettuce

Fresh parsley, chopped (for garnish)

In a large mixing bowl, combine the chopped apples, celery, grapes, toasted walnuts, and dried cranberries.

In a separate small bowl, whisk together the Greek yogurt, mayonnaise, lemon juice, honey, salt, and pepper until well combined. Taste and adjust the seasoning to your preference.

Pour the dressing over the apple mixture in the large bowl. Gently toss to coat all the ingredients evenly with the dressing. Cover the bowl with plastic wrap and refrigerate the Pfister Salad for at least 1 hour, allowing the flavors to meld together.

Wash and separate lettuce leaves. Gently pat dry and lay a leaf or two onto individual plates. Before serving, give the salad a gentle stir to redistribute the dressing. Scoop 1 generous cup of dressed salad onto the lettuce. Garnish with freshly chopped parsley (optional).

Serve on its own or with Wine-Soaked Roast Turkey and Gravy (page 123), Oven-Broasted Chicken (page 133), and TV Dinner Salisbury Steak (page 119).

Trivia

Ashley Pfister was portrayed by Linda Purl during season ten, but Purl had made a guest appearance on a previous episode. Who did she play?

Sandwiches

Morning at the Cunningham's isn't just breakfast. While Richie, Fonzie, Joanie, and Howard are eating, Marion is in the kitchen making sandwiches and putting together everyone's lunch for the day. She makes a dozen just for Chuck, because as Howard says, Chuck's appetite is larger than the entire country of Argentina. Here are favorites from the Cunningham's and Arnold's kitchens.

Homemade Honey-Cinnamon Peanut Butter *and* Raspberry Jam Sandwich

Whether crunchy or smooth, peanut butter and jelly is a lunchtime staple at the Cunninghams'. Richie prefers crunchy. Joanie likes smooth. Fonzie hates peanut butter and jelly sandwiches. What's a mom to do? If you're Marion Cunningham, you make everyone's favorites.

Honey-Cinnamon Peanut Butter

PREP TIME: *15 minutes* | YIELD: *10 to 12 ounces* | DIETARY NOTE: *Vegetarian, Gluten-Free*

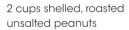

2 cups shelled, roasted unsalted peanuts

2 tablespoons honey

¼ teaspoon salt

½ teaspoon cinnamon

1 to 2 tablespoons peanut oil or other neutral oil (if needed)

Place the roasted unsalted peanuts in a food processor or high-powered blender. Process the peanuts for a few minutes until they start to break down and turn into a coarse crumb texture. Scrape down the sides of the food processor or blender as needed to ensure even processing.

Continue to process the peanuts until they reach a creamy consistency. This may take around 5 to 10 minutes (depending on the power of your appliance). Continue scraping down the sides as needed.

Add honey, salt, and cinnamon. Taste and add more honey, salt, and/or cinnamon as preferred.

Continue to process the mixture until the peanut butter becomes smooth and creamy. If the mixture seems too thick or dry, add 1 to 2 tablespoons of peanut oil or other neutral oil to achieve the desired consistency. Blend again until well incorporated.

Transfer the peanut butter to a clean jar or airtight container and store at room temperature. It will thicken slightly as it cools.

Quick Raspberry Jam

PREP TIME: *10 minutes* | SET TIME: *30 minutes* | YIELD: *four 8-ounce freezer-safe jars* | DIETARY NOTE: *Vegetarian, Vegan, Gluten-Free*

4 tablespoons instant pectin

2 cups granulated sugar

4 cups raspberries, rinsed

2 tablespoons bottled lemon juice

In a small bowl, combine the instant pectin with sugar. Stir well to ensure the pectin is evenly distributed. Set aside.

In a separate bowl, pour cleaned raspberries and mash into pulp. Add lemon juice and stir.

Add sugar-pectin mixture to raspberries and stir for 3 minutes.

Ladle mixture into four separate 8-ounce freezer-safe containers and set on counter to set for 30 minutes.

Once set, jam can be served. Store the remainder of the open jar in refrigerator and other jars in freezer for future use.

Peanut Butter and Jam Sandwiches

PREP TIME: *10 minutes* | **YIELD:** *1 sandwich per two slices of bread* | **DIETARY NOTE:** *Vegetarian*

2 slices "From the Store" Sandwich Bread (page 38) or *your* favorite from-the-store bread

1 to 2 tablespoons Honey-Cinnamon Peanut Butter (page 31)

1 tablespoon Quick Raspberry Jam (page 31)

Place slices of bread on a plate. Slather peanut butter to the edges of bread. Spread jam on top of peanut butter layer. Place other slice of bread on top. Cut diagonally.

NOTE

Blackberries, strawberries, and blueberries can be substituted for raspberries. And you can mix different berries together if the total amount as called for in recipe is the same.

Trivia

Peanut butter is thought of as a quintessential American food and made regular appearances on *Happy Days*. When did it become popular in the States?

Richie's Favorite Sardine Sandwich

What should one pack for a day at the Army recruitment office? Mrs. C. packed Richie his favorite lunch—something no one else would steal—a sardine sandwich! (Though someone stole his Twinkie.)

PREP TIME: *15 minutes* | **YIELD:** *2 sandwiches*

1 can sardines in olive oil, drained

¼ cup chopped fresh Italian parsley

2 tablespoons lemon juice

2 tablespoons extra virgin olive oil

¼ teaspoon kosher salt

⅛ teaspoon ground black pepper

4 slices crusty Italian bread or "From the Store" Sandwich Bread (page 38) or *your* favorite from-the-store bread

1 small red onion, thinly sliced

In a small bowl, mash the sardines gently with a fork to break them up into smaller pieces. Add the parsley, lemon juice, olive oil, salt, and pepper. Mix with fork until all ingredients are blended. Set aside to marinate.

Toast the slices of crusty Italian bread until they are lightly browned and crispy. Place the toasted bread slices on a clean surface or plate. Divide the sardine mixture among the bread slices, spreading it evenly.

Top the sardine mixture with sliced red onions, distributing them evenly over each sandwich. Place other slice of toasted bread on top and press down gently to hold sandwich together.

Serve immediately. Store any remaining sardine mixture in refrigerator.

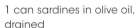

Trivia

Richie eventually served in the U.S. Army after he finished college. Where was he stationed after basic training?

Hawaiian Lūʻau Club Sandwich
with Secret Sandwich Spread

Richie throws the hippest lūʻau in town to celebrate Hawaii becoming a state. Instead of a pig roast on your front lawn, this hip-shakin' sandwich creates a mini-lūʻau in your lunchbox. You'll be limbo-ing in the lunchroom before eating the last bite.

PREP TIME: _20 minutes_ | **YIELD:** _1 sandwich_

2 slices SPAM®, fried, or 2 slices deli-style black forest ham

3 strips cooked bacon

3 slices Hawaiian-style sweet bread, toasted

1 to 2 tomato slices

1 slice canned ring pineapple

½ cup mayonnaise

¼ cup sweet chile sauce

1 to 2 leaves Bibb or Boston Lettuce

2 slices deli-style roast turkey

In a small frying pan, sear two thin slices of SPAM®. (Omit step if using black forest ham.) Cook bacon using preferred method (frying, baking, air-fryer, or microwave).

While SPAM® and bacon are cooking, toast bread, prepare tomato slices, and open and drain canned pineapple. Cut one ring in half.

For the Secret Sandwich Spread, in a small bowl mix the mayonnaise and chile sauce until evenly mixed. Place unused portions in a container and refrigerate.

Spread 1 tablespoon of Secret Sandwich Spread onto one slice of toasted bread. Place a leaf of lettuce on top, then strips of bacon, then tomato slices.

Spread another tablespoon of Secret Sandwich Spread onto toasted bread slice and place on top of sandwich stack. Place another lettuce leaf on top, then the slices of SPAM® or ham, then the pineapple half rings. Place the ends of the pineapple so they face the center of the sandwich so the Cunningham "C"s interlock for maximum pineapple coverage.

Place the turkey slices on top of the pineapple, then place final piece of toast on top of it all. Sandwich layers can be held together with a long toothpick, if desired.

Slice sandwich diagonally.

Trivia

Richie, Potsie, and Ralph meet a friend of Fonzie's, "Sticks" Downey, who wants to play drums with The Band. Why is he called "Sticks"?

"From the Store" Sandwich Bread

Marion is a full-time mom who bakes her own bread . . . except when she's too busy and needs Richie to buy a loaf of "from the store" bread. He's usually very helpful but tomorrow's lunch is in danger because Richie is busy figuring out how he and Potsie can see Bubbles the burlesque dancer!

PREP TIME: *30 minutes* | **RISE TIME:** *40 to 120 minutes* | **COOK TIME:** *about 40 minutes*
YIELD: *2 loaves of bread* | **DIETARY NOTE:** *Vegetarian, Vegan (with substitution)*

2 cups warm water (under 110°F)

2 tablespoons granulated sugar

2 packages active dry yeast

2 teaspoons sea or kosher salt

¼ cup warm melted butter (vegan substitute: vegetable oil)

6 to 6½ cups unbleached bread flour, divided*

NOTES

Substitute vegetable oil for butter throughout to make this bread vegan.

*The remaining 1½ cups of flour is used to cover work surface when kneading. You may not use all 1½ cups.

Trivia

When Richie and the guys finally see the legendary Bubbles, who else is at the show?

In a stoneware bowl mix water, sugar, and yeast. Stir to dissolve. Let stand for about 10 minutes (or until foamy). Add salt and butter; stir to mix. One cup at a time, add 5 cups of the flour, mixing thoroughly after each addition. Knead dough using one of these methods:

STAND-MIXER METHOD:
Move dough into mixer bowl with dough hook attachment. Turn on low setting. Let the dough hook work dough about 3 minutes.

HAND METHOD:
Move dough to lightly floured wood surface. Knead 6 to 8 minutes until dough is smooth and elastic.

Place dough into a lightly buttered stoneware bowl. Turn the dough over in bowl until it is fully coated with butter. Stretch plastic wrap over top of bowl. Let rise at room temperature until dough has tripled in bulk. The amount of time will vary depending on how warm and humid your kitchen is; about 20 to 60 minutes.

When dough has risen, remove plastic wrap and punch down dough. Divide the dough into 2 equal pieces and form each into a loaf shape. Place into two, buttered 9-by-5-inch loaf pans. Cover with plastic wrap and let rise until doubled, about 20 to 60 minutes.

Preheat oven to 450°F during last rise. Place a cookie sheet with about four ice cubes on the top oven rack. Place loaf pans on the lower rack. Bake for 10 minutes, then reduce the oven temperature to 350°F for about 30 minutes or until top of loaf is golden brown. Remove from the oven. Remove loaves from pans immediately and place on wire rack to cool. Fresh bread should be stored in a plastic bread bag and used within 4 days.

WHOLE-WHEAT VARIATION:
Instead of 6½ cups of bread flour, use 3½ cups bread flour and 3 cups whole wheat flour, mixed. (Five cups of flour mix is used for dough, the remaining 1½ cups for kneading.) Instead of sugar, use the same amount of honey.

RYE VARIATION:
Instead of 6½ cups of bread flour, use 3½ cups bread flour and 3 cups rye flour, mixed. (Five cups of flour mix is used for dough, the remaining 1½ cups for kneading.) Instead of sugar, use the same amount of honey. Mix in 2 tablespoons of caraway seeds to the flour mix before adding wet ingredients.

FROM **Arnold's** MENU

Fonzie teased Arnold that the food served wasn't actually good, but he always enjoyed a burger, especially ones made right after the grill was scrubbed. Cleanliness is important in the kitchen, but the perfect burger is always the second one made after the heat and meat have a chance to work their magic on the grill or frying pan.

THE BOPPER AND BIG BOPPER BURGERS

Maybe the secret to The Bopper Burger is a "seasoned" grill, but you can create the Arnold's experience at home when you serve these perfectamundo burgers.

PREP TIME: *15 minutes* | **CHILL TIME:** *30 minutes* | **COOK TIME:** *10 to 15 minutes* | **YIELD:** *4 burgers*

1 pound ground beef (80% lean, 20% fat)

½ pound ground round (90% to 95% lean, 5% to 10% fat)

1 tablespoon Worcestershire sauce

1 teaspoon Dijon mustard

1 teaspoon kosher salt

½ teaspoon freshly ground black pepper

4 tablespoons butter (half stick), separated into 4 pats

4 slices of your favorite cheese (cheddar, Gruyère, or blue cheese)

4 high-quality burger buns

4 lettuce leaves (butter lettuce or baby gem), separated and washed

4 tomato slices

1 red onion, thinly sliced, optional or add Fonzie's Favorite Fried Onions (page 42)

Pickles slices or chips, optional

Condiments (ketchup, mustard, and/or mayonnaise), optional

=== NOTE ===
To make Big Boppers—a double-decker burger—double all burger patty and toppings ingredients so each burger uses two patties.

In a large mixing bowl, combine the ground beef, ground round, Worcestershire sauce, Dijon mustard, kosher salt, and black pepper.

Gently mix the ingredients with your hands until well combined, being careful not to overwork the meat.

Divide the mixture into 4 equal portions and shape each portion into a patty, ensuring they are slightly larger than the burger buns.

Create a slight indentation in the center of each patty to prevent them from bulging during cooking.

Place the patties on a plate and refrigerate for at least 30 minutes to allow the flavors to meld.

Preheat a grill or skillet over medium-high heat.

Place burgers into hot skillet and place a pat of butter in the center of each patty.

Cook the burger patties for about 4 to 5 minutes, then carefully turn over the patty. Continue to cook for another 4 to 5 minutes, or until they reach your desired level of doneness.

During the last minute of cooking, place a slice of cheese on each patty and allow it to melt.

Remove the patties from the heat and let rest for a few minutes.

Recipe continues on next page

Trivia

Arnold's Burgers are named after who?

TO ASSEMBLE:

Slice the burger buns in half and lightly toast them on a grill or in a skillet until golden brown. Set aside and keep warm.

Take the bottom half of each toasted bun and spread mayonnaise or other optional condiment, if desired. Place a lettuce leaf on top of the mayonnaise, followed by a tomato slice and a few rings of raw red onion or Fonzie's Favorite Fried Onions.

Add the burger patty with melted cheese on top of the onion. If desired, add a dollop of ketchup, spread an even layer of mustard on the top half of the bun, and add a couple of pickles.

Finally, place the top half of bun on top of the burger.

 PAIRS WELL WITH French Fries (page 105) or Onion Rings (page 106) or a bag of everyone's favorite—potato chips!

FONZIE'S FAVORITE FRIED ONIONS

Have your burger Fonzie style: A Bopper with cheese and fried onions!

PREP TIME: *15 minutes* | **COOK TIME:** *20 to 30 minutes* | **YIELD:** *about 1 cup* | **DIETARY NOTE:** *Vegetarian, Gluten-Free*

2 large white or yellow onions

4 tablespoons (half stick) butter

Salt and gound black pepper to taste (about ½ teaspoon salt and ¼ teaspoon ground black pepper)

Peel the onions and cut them into thin slices between ¼ to ½ inch thick.

In a large sauté pan, melt the butter over medium heat. Swirl the pan to evenly coat the surface with the melted butter.

Add the sliced onions to the pan and spread them out into an even layer. Add salt and black pepper.

Cook the onions slowly over medium-low heat, stirring occasionally to prevent sticking and ensure even cooking.

Allow the onions to cook for about 20 to 30 minutes or until they soften and turn golden brown. Adjust the heat as needed to prevent burning.

Remove the sauté pan from the heat and transfer the fried onions to a storage dish or use them immediately for your hamburger topping.

HOT DIGGITY DOG AND DADDY-O DOG

The Hot Diggity and Daddy-O Dogs have been on Arnold's menu since, well, Arnold! Perfect for every occasion, but these worked especially well when Al set up a hot dog stand on the Cunningham's lawn. His setup provided sustenance for the spectacle of watching Fonzie get his beard shaved off to start a new job as the auto-mechanic teacher at Jefferson High School.

PREP TIME: 20 minutes | **COOK TIME:** 8 to 10 minutes | **YIELD:** 4 servings

4 beef hot dogs

4 high-quality hot dog buns

1 tablespoon vegetable oil

FOR THE TOPPINGS (OPTIONAL):

Yellow mustard

Ketchup

Sweet pickle relish

Chopped onions

Chopped tomatoes

Preheat grill or a skillet over medium heat. If using a skillet, add vegetable oil to coat the pan. If using a grill, lightly brush vegetable oil onto the grate.

Place the hot dog buns on the grill or skillet to lightly toast them. Remove and set aside once toasted.

Grill or cook the hot dogs until the outside is lightly browned and crispy and the hot dogs are heated through.

Spread a stripe of yellow mustard, if desired, along the inside of each toasted hot dog bun.

Place cooked hot dog in the bun. Add desired toppings, such as ketchup, sweet pickle relish, chopped onions, and chopped tomatoes. Substitute Fonzie's Favorite Fried Onions (page 42) for the chopped onions, if desired. Serve immediately.

A Hot Diggity Dog is transformed into a Daddy-O Dog when, instead of condiments and toppings, ¼ to ½ cup of Arnold's Slow Cooker Chili (page 45) is slathered on top of the cooked hot dog.

ARNOLD'S SLOW COOKER CHILI

Turn your Hot Diggity Dog into a Daddy-O Dog. Or just enjoy the chili and 86 the dog!

PREP TIME: *20 minutes* | **COOK TIME:** *3 to 4 hours* | **YIELD:** *6 to 8 servings*

1 tablespoon vegetable oil

1 pound ground beef (85% lean, 15% fat)

8 ounces lager or ale style beer or 8 ounces beef broth

1 white onion, finely chopped

2 garlic cloves, minced

1 red bell pepper, finely chopped

1 jalapeño pepper, finely chopped (optional, for heat)

1 tablespoon tomato paste

One 14-ounce can diced tomatoes

One 15-ounce can kidney beans, drained and rinsed

1 tablespoon chile powder

1 teaspoon ground cumin

1 teaspoon paprika

½ teaspoon dried oregano

Salt and ground black pepper, to taste

Heat vegetable oil in a large skillet over medium heat. Add the ground beef and beer (or broth) to the pan and cook, breaking large chunks into smaller pieces with a spoon, until browned and cooked through.

Pour beef mixture into crockpot. Add the chopped onion, minced garlic, red bell pepper, and jalapeño pepper. Stir in the tomato paste and diced tomatoes, kidney beans, chile powder, ground cumin, paprika, dried oregano, salt, and pepper. Stir well to combine all the ingredients.

Set crockpot/slow cooker to high setting and cook for one hour. Stir after an hour and set to low.

Continue cooking for another hour. Check for spiciness, add more chile powder if desired.

Remove cover and cook for another 30 to 60 minutes until chili is at desired consistency.

Simmer longer with cover on to further develop the flavors. Stir occasionally as it cooks on a low setting.

Ladle over hot dog as prepared in Hot Diggity Dog (page 43) recipe.

Trivia

Why did Fonzie have a beard?

MOMO BURGERS

The gang is surprised when Arnold announces he's getting married. The beautiful Momo is coming from Japan after years of exchanging love letters with her unlikely fiancé. Arnold is the happiest anyone has ever seen him—he even declares he's naming a burger after his new bride! It's the Momo Burger; we hope she likes it.

PREP TIME: *20 minutes* | **COOK TIME:** *8 to 10 minutes* | **YIELD:** *4 burgers*

¾ pound ground turkey

¾ pound ground pork

¼ cup finely chopped white onion

2 garlic cloves, minced

1 teaspoon fresh ginger, grated

1 teaspoon ground cumin

1 teaspoon ground coriander

½ teaspoon turmeric

½ teaspoon ancho chile powder

½ teaspoon salt

¼ teaspoon ground black pepper

2 tablespoons fresh cilantro, finely chopped

1 tablespoon vegetable oil

Burger buns

Optional toppings: Lettuce, tomato slices, red onion slices, mayonnaise, ketchup, mustard, or any of your preferred burger toppings.

In a large mixing bowl, combine the ground turkey, ground pork, chopped onion, minced garlic, grated ginger, ground cumin, ground coriander, turmeric, ancho chile powder, salt, black pepper, and fresh cilantro. Mix well to combine all the ingredients.

Divide the mixture into 4 equal portions and shape each portion into a patty, ensuring they are slightly larger than the burger buns.

Heat the vegetable oil in a skillet or grill pan over medium heat.

Cook the burger patties in the preheated skillet for about 4 to 5 minutes per side, or until they are cooked through and reach an internal temperature of 165°F. While the patties are cooking, you can toast the burger buns if desired.

When patties are cooked, remove them from the skillet and let them rest for a couple of minutes.

TO ASSEMBLE:

Take the bottom half of each toasted bun and spread mayonnaise. Place a lettuce leaf on top of the mayonnaise, followed by a tomato slice and a few rings of raw red onion or Fonzie's Favorite Fried Onions (page 42).

Add the Momo patty on top of the onion. Add a dollop of ketchup and any other condiments. Try the spread used in the Hawaiian Lūʻau Club Sandwich with Secret Sandwich Spread (page 36)! Finally, place the top half of bun on top of the burger.

Trivia

Fonzie is asked to be Arnold's best man, but he can't because of the Fonzarelli Curse. What's the Fonzarelli Curse?

THE BIG "A" SLOPPY JOE SANDWICH

Arnold passed his secret recipe for the Big "A" to Big Al Delvecchio and now it's in your hands. Make a batch and have sandwiches for a crowd of hungry teenagers.

PREP TIME: *20 minutes* | **COOK TIME:** *1½ to 2 hours* | **YIELD:** *10 to 12 sandwiches*

2 tablespoons butter (margarine can be substituted)

1 medium yellow or white onion, diced

½ cup chopped celery

1 teaspoon minced garlic

1½ pounds ground round beef (85% to 90% lean, 15% to 10% fat)

1½ pounds ground chuck beef (80% lean, 20% fat)

One 8-ounce can condensed tomato soup

1 cup ketchup

2 tablespoons cider vinegar

2 tablespoons Worcestershire sauce

3 tablespoons brown sugar (light or dark)

1 teaspoon dried mustard powder

½ teaspoon ground black pepper

½ teaspoon salt

Pretzel or brioche buns

Preheat oven to 300°F.

In a large frying pan over medium-high heat, melt the butter. Add the onion, celery, and garlic, and sauté until lightly browned and glistening. Transfer the sautéed mixture to a large casserole baking dish and set aside.

In the same frying pan, add both ground beef and cook until browned, breaking the meat into smaller chunks using a spatula.

Drain any excess liquid from the meat, then add it to the casserole dish with the onion, celery, and garlic mixture.

Add the condensed tomato soup, ketchup, cider vinegar, Worcestershire sauce, brown sugar, dried mustard powder, black pepper, and salt to the casserole dish. Mix thoroughly to combine all the ingredients.

Cover the casserole dish and bake for 1½ to 2 hours, or until the edges of the mixture are lightly bubbling.

To serve, spoon the Sloppy Joe mixture onto pretzel or brioche buns.

=== NOTE ===

For a spicier version, add 1 teaspoon to 1 tablespoon of your favorite hot pepper sauce and ¼ cup to ½ cup of sliced pickled or canned jalapeño peppers. To make vegetarian, swap the ground beef for your favorite "beef" crumbles and use tamari sauce instead of Worcestershire sauce.

Trivia

Al Delvecchio, before finding true love with Louisa Arcola, pined for a former sweetheart. What was her name?

DELUX B.L.T.

Think all bacon-lettuce-tomato sandwiches are the same? You haven't tried this one! Clarence the cook would approve of the secret ingredient that makes this version of Arnold's Delux B.L.T. so very salty, crispy, and delicious.

PREP TIME: *15 minutes* | **YIELD:** *1 sandwich*

6 strips cooked bacon

3 slices "From the Store" Sandwich Bread (page 38) or *your* favorite from-the-store bread

1 tablespoon mayonnaise

2 to 4 leaves iceberg lettuce

2 to 4 slices beefsteak tomato

2 to 4 kosher dill pickle, sandwich slices

1 tablespoon unsweetened peanut butter

Cook bacon using preferred method (frying, baking, air fryer, or microwave). Toast bread. Thinly slice tomato. Select and wash bread-sized lettuce pieces. Set aside.

Place a slice of toasted bread onto a plate. Spread 1 tablespoon of mayonnaise, place lettuce leaf on top, then 3 strips of bacon, then 1 or 2 slices of tomato. Place lettuce leaf on top, then 1 to 2 slices of pickle, then remaining bacon, then 1 to 2 slices of tomato. On the second toasted slice of bread, spread peanut butter evenly to edges of bread. Place the final piece of toasted bread on top.

Note: Alternate stacking direction of bacon and pickle slices for a sturdier sandwich. Sandwich layers can be held together with a long toothpick, if needed. Slice sandwich diagonally.

Trivia

Arnold's Drive-In employed four cooks throughout the run of the show. Who were they?

SPLISH-SPLASH TUNA MELT SANDWICH

Richie, Potsie, and Ralph have a hard time keeping a drummer, but they can play the hits! For their big show at the Leopard Lodge dance, they bring everyone to the dance floor with a rollicking rendition of this sandwich's namesake, "Splish Splash." Mr. Cunningham said the lyrics made no sense, but the kids know that splishin' and splashin' is what you'll do when you see this sandwich on your plate.

PREP TIME: *15 minutes* | **COOK TIME:** *6 to 8 minutes* | **YIELD:** *1 sandwich*

One 5-ounce can tuna in water, drained

2 tablespoons mayonnaise

1 tablespoon Dijon mustard

¼ cup diced celery

¼ cup diced red onion

Pinch of salt, to taste

Pinch of ground black pepper, to taste

Butter, softened

4 slices "From the Store" Sandwich Bread (page 38) or *your* favorite from-the-store bread

2 to 4 slices cheese (cheddar, Swiss, or your favorite melting cheese)

In a medium-sized mixing bowl, combine the drained tuna, mayonnaise, Dijon mustard, diced celery, and diced red onion. Mix well to combine.

Season the tuna mixture with salt and pepper to taste.

Preheat a skillet or griddle over medium heat.

Butter one side of each slice of bread. Place one slice of bread, butter-side down, onto the preheated skillet. Spoon the tuna mixture onto the bread and spread it evenly.

Top the tuna mixture with the cheese slices. (Add 2 slices for regular cheesy or 4 slices for extra cheesy.) Place the second slice of bread, butter-side up, on top of the cheese to form a sandwich.

Cook the sandwich for about 3 to 4 minutes on each side, or until the bread turns golden brown and the cheese is melted. Press the sandwich gently with a spatula to help melt the cheese. Once the sandwich is cooked to your liking, remove it from the skillet and transfer it to a cutting board.

Allow the sandwich to cool for a minute or two before slicing it in half.

Trivia

What was the name of Richie, Potsie, and Ralph's band?

GRILLED CHEESE WITH PEANUTS

Comfort food at its finest! While you may not be able to find farmer Vernon Boompergaard's award-winning cheese or make out with the Boompergaard twins, Inga and Helga, you can make your own happiness with Arnold's hammy grilled cheese. Don't forget the peanuts!

PREP TIME: *20 minutes* | **COOK TIME:** *1½ to 2 hours* | **YIELD:** *10 to 12 sandwiches*

Dijon mustard, to taste

8 slices "From the Store" Sandwich Bread (page 38) or *your* favorite from-the-store bread

8 slices Swiss or Gruyère cheese

8 slices deli-style ham (optional)

Pinch of salt, to taste

Pinch of ground black pepper, to taste

4 tablespoons unsalted butter, softened

2 cups salted, roasted peanuts

Preheat a skillet or griddle over medium heat.

Spread a thin layer of Dijon mustard on one side of each slice of bread. Place 2 slices of cheese on the mustard side of 4 bread slices. Season with a pinch of salt and pepper. (If using ham, add 2 slices of ham between the cheese slices.)

Place the remaining 4 slices of bread on top, mustard-side down. Spread softened butter on the outer sides of each sandwich.

Place the sandwiches in the preheated skillet or griddle and cook until golden brown and the cheese has melted, about 3 to 4 minutes per side.

Press down gently on the sandwiches with a spatula while cooking to ensure even browning and melting of the cheese. Once the sandwiches are golden brown and the cheese is melted, remove them from the skillet or griddle.

Let the sandwiches rest for a minute before cutting them in half diagonally. Serve each sandwich with ½ cup of peanuts, just like Arnold's!

=== NOTE ===

Forget the peanuts to easily adjust this recipe if you have a peanut allergy.

Trivia

Fonzie and Richie are on a mission while visiting Lake Pinewood—meet the lonely farmer's daughters, Inga and Helga. How did they sneak past Farmer Boompergaard?

Snacks and Lunchbox Treats

It's 3 p.m. and dinner is still three hours away. Time for a snack!
But don't eat too much or you'll spoil your appetite. Mrs.
Cunningham has been working all day on that meatloaf.

Fonzie's Mom's Cinnamon Shortbread Cookies

Dear to Fonzie's heart are the three remaining cookies in his mom's cookie jar. How long have they been in the jar? Thirty years! These cinnamon shortbread cookies keep for a long time, but not thirty years long.

PREP TIME: *30 minutes total* | **COOK TIME:** *about 45 minutes* | **YIELD:** *about 16 cookies* | **DIETARY NOTE:** *Vegetarian*

2¼ cup cake flour

½ teaspoon cinnamon plus 1 teaspoon

½ teaspoon kosher salt, fine

½ cup (1 stick) salted, high-fat butter (82% to 84% butterfat)

½ cup extra-fine sugar plus 2 teaspoons

1 teaspoon vanilla extract

2 teaspoons extra fine sugar

1 teaspoon cinnamon

NOTE

Extra-fine sugar can be purchased, or you can use a food processor to transform granulated sugar into extra fine. Extra-fine sugar is not the same as powdered sugar and cannot be substituted.

Preheat oven to 325°F.

Sift together flour, cinnamon, and salt into large bowl. Set aside.

In another bowl, cream butter and sugar. Add vanilla and beat until thoroughly mixed.

Add the butter mixture to the flour mixture and, using pastry cutter, combine until texture is crumbly yet holds together.

Fit parchment paper into a 9-by-9-inch cake pan. Press dough into pan, making sure to evenly distribute.

Combine 2 teaspoons of sugar and 1 teaspoon of cinnamon in a small bowl until thoroughly mixed. Sprinkle evenly on top of dough.

Place in the oven and bake until the top is slightly browned, approximately 45 minutes. Remove from the oven and cool in pan for 15 minutes.

Carefully remove contents (use the parchment edges as a sling) and place onto cutting board. (It will still be warm, be careful!) Using a large butcher knife or cleaver, cut into 2-inch squares. Place onto wire rack to cool completely.

Serve when cooled. Store in covered container for approximately a week. Freezes well.

Malachi Crunch Spicy Snack Mix

Myron "The Count" Malachi and his brother Rocco are a couple of no-good hoods! They wreck Pinky's car then give her the Malachi Crunch, sending her straight to the hospital. This Malachi Crunch won't smash your car but will raise your temperature. Release the pigeons!

PREP TIME: *20 minutes total* | **COOK TIME:** *about 45 minutes* | **YIELD:** *about 15 cups*

- 3 cups crunchy corn square cereal
- 3 cups crunchy rice square cereal
- 3 cups crunchy wheat square cereal
- 1 cup bagel chips
- 1 cup garlic-rye chips
- 2 cups bite-sized pretzels
- 1 cup roasted, salted peanuts
- 1 cup hot and crunchy cheesy corn puff snacks
- 8 tablespoons (1 stick) unsalted butter
- 2 tablespoons Worcestershire sauce
- 2 teaspoons seasoned salt
- 1½ teaspoons garlic powder
- 1 teaspoon onion powder
- ½ teaspoon smoked paprika
- ½ to 1 teaspoon ghost pepper powder (or other hot pepper powder)

Measure and pour dry all the cereals, bagel and garlic-rye chips, pretzels, peanuts, and corn puff snacks into a large bowl and mix with wooden spoon until all ingredients are evenly distributed. Set aside.

Preheat oven to 250°F.

Melt butter in a large (32-ounce) microwave-safe bowl. Melt in 20-second increments, stirring after each interval, until butter is melted but not boiling.

Add the remaining ingredients and whisk together until thoroughly blended.

Pour over the snack mix you put aside and carefully stir with wooden spoon until all pieces are coated. Mix together with latex/plastic gloved hands. Do not touch with bare hands as pepper powder can cause a reaction or burn to skin.

Line baking sheets with parchment paper. Split the mixture between the two baking sheets and spread out evenly. Place into the oven and bake until lightly browned and crispy, approximately 45 minutes. Gently turn over the mixture on the baking sheet every 15 minutes. Let cool for 10 minutes.

When entirely cooled, transfer any unused Malachi Crunch to sealed storage container. Keeps for up to 4 weeks.

NOTE

You can adjust the heat levels by adding more hot pepper powder or pepper powder from a hotter pepper, like Carolina Reapers. Whatever you do, use safety when handling hot peppers. Do not let the pepper powder come into contact with your skin and wash your hands before touching any sensitive body parts. This recipe can be made vegetarian by substituting Worcestershire sauce with tamari.

Trivia
What kind of car does Pinky drive in the demolition derby?

Jump the Shark Candy Sushi

Would you jump over a shark on your motorcycle? One slip and it's chomp, chomp! Turn the tables on the California Kid (and the shark) with this irreverent treat that lets you do the chomping.

PREP TIME: *40 minutes* | **CHILL TIME:** *15 minutes* | **COOK TIME:** *10 to 15 minutes* | **YIELD:** *about 20 individual pieces*

½ cup (1 stick) butter or margarine

4 cups miniature marshmallows

6 cups crispy rice cereal

1 bag gummy shark candy

1 box green-colored fruit roll-ups (If you can't find green, use your favorite color.)

1 to 2 cups shredded coconut

4 to 6 drops blue food coloring

Trivia

What were the Cunninghams and the gang doing in Hollywood?

In a large stock pot, melt butter over low heat. Add marshmallows, and gently stir with wooden spoon until mixture is smooth. Remove from heat.

Add crispy rice cereal to stock pot and stir until evenly mixed.

Line jelly roll pan with parchment paper. Carefully—mixture is hot—fill pan. Cover the surface with a piece of waxed paper and press mixture evenly into pan. Cool for 15 minutes.

While crispy rice mixture is cooling, set up a clear 24-by-24-inch counter workspace and cover with waxed paper. Open candy bag and place into small bowls. Unroll a sheet of fruit roll-ups and flatten onto a small cutting board. Cut approximately twelve 1-by-4-inch strips and set aside.

Add ½ cup of shredded coconut to plastic bag. Add 2 drops of food dye. Add the rest of coconut and 2 more drops of food dye. Seal bag and gently squish around until dye is distributed. (Uneven coloring is okay as it will better resemble the color gradient of water.) On a metal pie tin, sprinkle shredded coconut until pie tin is filled. Set aside to dry.

Assemble the sushi: First, turn the cooled crispy rice mixture onto the covered counter and cut in half, lengthwise. Place one half back into pan and set aside.

Cut the other half into 2-by-3-inch rectangles. Place shark gummy on crispy rice rectangle, gently pressing down. Take a strip of cut fruit leather and wrap around crispy rice and shark in the middle. (Overlap fruit leather if necessary.) Place completed candy sushi onto shredded coconut in pie tin. Repeat until finished.

Serve immediately or store in an air-tight container for up to 3 days.

Fig Bar Cookies

Fig Bar Cookies are more than delicious, they're medicinal! Fonzie keeps a supply close at hand to help with everything from insomnia to Potsie's nerves before a big exam. As Fonz says, take two, one for now and one for later.

PREP TIME: *20 minutes* | **CHILL TIME:** *60 minutes* | **COOK TIME:** *15 to 20 minutes*
YIELD: *about 2 dozen cookies* | **DIETARY NOTE:** *Vegetarian*

1¾ cups all-purpose flour

½ teaspoon baking powder

¼ teaspoon salt

½ cup unsalted butter, softened

½ cup granulated sugar

1 large egg

1 teaspoon vanilla extract

1½ cups dried figs, stemmed

½ cup water

2 tablespoons honey

½ teaspoon lemon zest

1 tablespoon lemon juice

Trivia

Potsie had a difficult time remembering facts and details needed for his anatomy exam and is frustrated. How does The Fonz help Potsie?

In a medium bowl, whisk together the flour, baking powder, and salt. Set aside.

In a large mixing bowl, cream together the softened butter and granulated sugar until light and fluffy. This can be done with an electric mixer or by hand using a wooden spoon. Beat in the egg and vanilla extract until well combined.

Gradually add the dry ingredients to the butter mixture, mixing until just combined. Avoid overmixing.

Divide the dough into 2 equal portions and shape each portion into a rectangular block. Wrap each block in plastic wrap and refrigerate for at least 1 hour or until firm.

While the dough is chilling, prepare the fig filling: In a small saucepan, combine the dried figs, water, honey, lemon zest, and lemon juice. Bring the mixture to a simmer over medium heat and cook for about 10 minutes, or until the figs are softened and the mixture thickens. Remove from heat and let it cool.

Preheat oven to 350°F. Line a baking sheet with parchment paper.

On a lightly floured surface, roll out one portion of the dough into a rectangular shape, about ¼ inch thick.

Spread half of the fig filling evenly over the rolled-out dough, leaving a small border around the edges.

Carefully roll the dough, starting from one of the long sides, into a log shape. Repeat the process with the remaining dough and fig filling.

Place the rolled logs onto the prepared baking sheet and gently flatten them slightly with the palm of your hand.

Bake for 15 to 20 minutes, or until the edges are lightly golden.

Remove from the oven and let the logs cool on the baking sheet for about 10 minutes.

Transfer the logs to a cutting board and slice them into individual cookie bars, about 1 inch thick.

Allow the fig bars to cool completely on a wire rack before serving.

Store the homemade fig bars in an airtight container at room temperature for up to a week.

Potato Chip Cookies

Salty and crunchy! Potato chips were a staple in the Cunningham house. When Marion heard about using potato chips in cookies from the gals at the Leopard Lodge Ladies Auxiliary, she knew Howard and Richie would love them.

PREP TIME: *20 minutes* | **COOK TIME:** *about 45 minutes* | **YIELD:** *about 30 cookies* | **DIETARY NOTE:** *Vegetarian*

- 1 cup unsalted butter, softened
- ½ cup granulated sugar
- ½ cup packed light brown sugar
- 1 teaspoon vanilla extract
- 2 cups all-purpose flour
- 1 cup crushed potato chips
- ½ cup chopped pecans or walnuts (optional)
- ½ teaspoon baking soda
- ¼ teaspoon salt

Preheat oven to 350°F and line baking sheets with parchment paper.

In a large mixing bowl, cream together the softened butter, granulated sugar, and brown sugar until light and fluffy. Stir in the vanilla extract until well combined.

In a separate bowl, whisk together the flour, crushed potato chips, chopped pecans or walnuts (if using), baking soda, and salt.

Gradually add the dry ingredient mixture to the butter and sugar mixture, stirring until just combined. Don't overmix.

Drop rounded tablespoonfuls of cookie dough onto the prepared baking sheets, spacing them about 2 inches apart.

Flatten each cookie slightly with the back of a spoon.

Place baking sheets in the oven and bake for 10 to 12 minutes, or until the edges are lightly golden.

Remove the baking sheets from the oven and let the cookies cool on the sheets for a few minutes before transferring them to a wire rack to cool completely.

Store them in an airtight container at room temperature for up to 1 week.

Granny Nussbaum's Sweets

Fonzie wears his heart on his sleeve for only one lady: Grandma Nussbaum! She's always ready with a sweet snack for her little Skippy. But don't worry, she hasn't made a peanut butter and relish sandwich in years. That would be wrrr, wrrr, wrrrong!

Apple Snack Cake

Grandma Nussbaum remembers this recipe as a favorite of her first husband, Mr. Fonzarelli.

PREP TIME: *30 minutes total* | **COOK TIME:** *35 to 40 minutes* | **YIELD:** *about 16 squares* | **DIETARY NOTE:** *Vegetarian*

2 cups all-purpose flour

1½ teaspoons baking powder

½ teaspoon baking soda

½ teaspoon ground cinnamon

¼ teaspoon ground nutmeg

¼ teaspoon salt

½ cup unsalted butter, softened

1 cup granulated sugar

2 large eggs

1 teaspoon 100% pure vanilla extract

½ cup sour cream

2 cups peeled and diced apples (about 2 medium-sized apples, your favorite variety)

Powdered sugar for dusting (optional)

Preheat oven to 350°F. Line a 9-by-9-inch baking pan with parchment paper.

In a medium-sized bowl, whisk together the flour, baking powder, baking soda, cinnamon, nutmeg, and salt. Set aside.

In a large mixing bowl, cream together the softened butter and granulated sugar until light and fluffy. This can be done with an electric mixer or by hand using a wooden spoon. Beat in the eggs, one at a time, followed by the vanilla extract.

Gradually add the dry ingredients to the butter mixture, alternating with the sour cream. Begin and end with the dry ingredients, mixing each addition until just combined. Avoid overmixing.

Gently fold in the diced apples, ensuring they are evenly distributed throughout the batter.

Pour the batter into the prepared baking pan and spread it out evenly.

Place pans into the oven and bake for 35 to 40 minutes, or until a toothpick inserted into the center comes out clean.

Remove the cake from the oven and let it cool in the pan for about 10 minutes. Then, transfer it to a wire rack to cool completely.

Once the cake has cooled, dust with powdered sugar for a decorative touch. Cut the apple snack cake into squares or slices. It's delicious on its own but terrific with a dollop of whipped cream or a scoop of Arnold's World-Famous Frozen Soft-Serve Custard (page 165).

NOTE

This apple snack cake can be stored in an airtight container at room temperature for up to 3 days.

Trivia

Mr. Nussbaum? Which husband was that, Grandma?

Old-Fashioned Chocolate Chip Cookies

Grandma Nussbaum was just as cool as Fonzie; she even learned how to make these new-fangled cookies in 1938 for husband number two.

PREP TIME: *30 minutes* | **CHILL TIME:** *24 to 72 hours* | **COOK TIME:** *12 to 14 minutes*
YIELD: *about 24 large cookies* | **DIETARY NOTE:** *Vegetarian*

2 cups cake flour

1⅔ cups bread flour

1¼ teaspoon baking soda

1½ teaspoons baking powder

1½ teaspoons kosher salt

1¼ cups (2½ sticks) unsalted butter, at room temperature

1¼ cup dark brown sugar

1 cup granulated white sugar

2 eggs

2 teaspoons 100% vanilla extract

1 cup dark chocolate chips

1 cup semi-sweet chocolate chips

1 cup milk chocolate chips

Sift together the cake flour, bread flour, baking soda, baking powder, and salt into a large bowl, and set aside.

Cream together butter and sugars on medium speed until very light, about 5 minutes. Add the eggs one at a time, mixing well after each addition, then add the vanilla. Reduce the mixer speed to low, gradually add the dry ingredients and mix until just combined, 5 to 10 seconds.

Using a rubber spatula, fold in the chocolate chips.

Press plastic wrap against the dough and refrigerate for at least 24 hours and up to 72 hours.

When ready to bake, preheat oven to 350°F. Line a baking sheet with parchment paper.

Scoop a tablespoon of dough and roll into a rough ball (it should be the size of a large golf ball) and place on the baking sheet. Repeat until you have six mounds of dough on the cookie sheet.

Bake until golden brown but still soft, 12 to 14 minutes.

Remove from the oven and cool on the pan for 10 minutes then transfer the cookies onto another cooling rack to cool a bit more, until just warm or at room temperature. Repeat with remaining dough.

Store leftover cookies in an airtight container at room temperature for up to 3 days. Freezes well.

Rugelach

Don't wait for the High Holidays! Enjoy Granny's Rugelach any time of year.

PREP TIME: *30 minutes* | **CHILL TIME:** *60 minutes total* | **COOK TIME:** *18 to 20 minutes*
YIELD: *32 pieces* | **DIETARY NOTE:** *Vegetarian*

2 cups all-purpose flour

¼ teaspoon kosher salt

1 cup (2 sticks) unsalted butter, cold and cut into small pieces

8 ounces cream cheese, cold and cut into small pieces

¼ cup granulated sugar

1 teaspoon vanilla extract

1 cup finely chopped nuts (such as walnuts, pecans, or almonds)

½ cup packed brown sugar

1½ teaspoons ground cinnamon

½ cup fruit preserves (such as raspberry, apricot, or strawberry)

2 tablespoons unsalted butter, melted

2 tablespoons granulated sugar

1 teaspoon ground cinnamon

In a large mixing bowl, combine the flour and salt. Add the cold butter and cream cheese. Use a pastry cutter to cut the butter and cream cheese into the flour until the mixture resembles coarse crumbs.

Add the granulated sugar and vanilla extract to the dough mixture. Mix until the dough comes together. Divide the dough into 4 equal portions and shape each portion into a disk. Wrap each disk in plastic wrap and refrigerate for at least 1 hour, or until the dough is firm.

Preheat oven to 350°F. Line baking sheets with parchment paper.

In a small bowl, mix the finely chopped nuts, brown sugar, and ground cinnamon to make the filling.

Take one portion of the dough out of the refrigerator and roll it out on a lightly floured surface into a circle about ⅛ inch thick. Spread about 2 tablespoons of fruit preserves over the rolled-out dough, leaving a small border around the edges. Sprinkle a quarter of the nut filling evenly over the preserves.

Using a sharp knife or pizza cutter, cut the dough circle into 8 wedges. Starting from the wider end, roll up each wedge tightly, like a crescent roll. Place the rolled rugelach on the prepared baking sheet, point-side down, and repeat the process with the remaining dough and filling.

Brush each rugelach with melted butter and sprinkle with a mixture of granulated sugar and ground cinnamon.

Bake the rugelach for 18 to 20 minutes, or until they turn golden brown. Remove from the oven and transfer to a wire rack to cool completely.

Repeat the process with the remaining dough and filling until all the rugelach is baked.

Once the rugelach has cooled, they are ready to be eaten. Store them in an airtight container at room temperature for up to 1 week.

NOTE

Rugelach is a versatile treat, and you can customize the filling by adding ingredients like chocolate chips, dried fruit, or even a sprinkle of cinnamon sugar.

Drinks

Nothing beats a refreshing beverage after a long day of school, work, or cruising around. Whether you're hosting a sock hop, mowing the lawn, or hanging out with the gang playing Twister, these drinks hit the spot.

Holiday Cider Punch

Harvest Balls, Thanksgiving, Homecoming, or a family bonfire . . . there's always a reason to get together with a big bowl of punch. Pop popcorn, toast a few marshmallows, pour a cup of cider punch and Uncle Joe will tell us a story of Cousin Cecil Cunningham who battled rum-running gangsters in the 1920s.

PREP TIME: *30 minutes active* | **CHILL TIME:** *1 to 2 hours* | **YIELD:** *about 8 to 10 servings* | **DIETARY NOTE:** *Vegetarian, Gluten-Free*

4 cups apple cider

2 cups cranberry juice

1 cup orange juice

¼ cup lemon juice

¼ cup honey (adjust to taste)

2 cinnamon sticks

4 to 6 whole cloves

1 apple, thinly sliced

1 orange, thinly sliced

Ice cubes

Sparkling water or ginger ale, chilled (optional)

Fresh cranberries and mint leaves for garnish (optional)

In a large punch bowl or pitcher, combine the apple cider, cranberry juice, orange juice, lemon juice, and honey. Stir well until the honey is dissolved.

Add the cinnamon sticks and whole cloves to the punch mixture, giving it a gentle stir.

Add the thinly sliced apple and orange to the punch, reserving some for garnish if desired.

Refrigerate the punch for at least 1 hour to allow the flavors to meld together.

Just before serving, add ice cubes to the punch to keep it chilled. If a bubbly punch is preferred, add sparkling water or ginger ale to the mix. Start with about 1 cup and adjust to your taste preference. Give the punch a final stir to incorporate any added carbonated beverage.

Serve the cider punch in glasses or cups filled with ice cubes. Garnish each glass with fresh cranberries, mint leaves, and slices of apple and orange if desired.

Trivia

Which real-life gangsters would Cousin Cecil have been fighting?

"Spiked" Orange Eggnog

Mrs. C. makes a few batches of nog during the cold and snowy winter because Mr. C. loves it after shoveling all that snow. We don't recommend drinking seventy-two teeny-weenie glasses—it's spiked!

PREP TIME: *20 minutes* | **COOK TIME:** *12 to 14 minutes* | **CHILL TIME:** *about 2 hours*
YIELD: *about 5 to 6 servings* | **DIETARY NOTE:** *Vegetarian, Gluten-Free*

4 large eggs

½ cup granulated sugar

2 cups whole milk

1 cup heavy cream

½ cup freshly squeezed orange juice

1 tablespoon orange zest

1 teaspoon vanilla extract

¼ teaspoon ground nutmeg

½ cup spiced rum or bourbon (optional)

Orange slices and nutmeg for garnish (optional)

NOTE

If you prefer a non-alcoholic version, you can omit the spiced rum or bourbon.

Trivia

Eggnog was a popular winter holiday beverage during the *Happy Days* era and is related to another milk punch that inspired a feuding cat and mouse. What is it?

In a large mixing bowl, whisk together the eggs and sugar until well combined and slightly frothy.

In a saucepan, heat the milk and heavy cream over medium heat until it begins to steam. Do not let it boil.

Slowly pour about ½ cup of the hot milk mixture into the egg mixture while whisking continuously. This will temper the eggs and prevent them from curdling.

Gradually pour the tempered egg mixture back into the saucepan with the remaining hot milk, whisking constantly.

Cook the mixture over medium heat, stirring constantly, until it thickens and coats the back of a spoon. This should take about 5 to 7 minutes. Do not let it boil.

Remove the saucepan from heat and stir in the orange juice, orange zest, vanilla extract, and ground nutmeg. Mix well to combine.

Allow the mixture to cool to room temperature, then cover and refrigerate for at least 2 hours or until chilled. Once chilled, give the orange eggnog a good stir. If it has thickened too much, you can whisk in a little more milk to achieve the desired consistency.

Stir in the spiced rum or bourbon into the chilled orange eggnog. Adjust the amount to your preference, adding more or less depending on how strong you want the alcohol flavor.

Pour the orange eggnog into serving glasses. Garnish each glass with a sprinkle of ground nutmeg and a slice of orange, if desired.

"Sugar Lips" Smoothie

The Fonz needs a few days of smoothies after a visit to the dentist to get his kisser back in shape, but you don't need a tooth pulled to enjoy one anytime. Same for *Fonsillectomies*; it only comes out once, but you don't have to tell anyone you've already had it removed to drink this smoothie. Double the batch for Fonzie, pleasey-weasy.

PREP TIME: *15 minutes active* | **YIELD:** *one 16-ounce smoothie* | **DIETARY NOTE:** *Vegetarian, Gluten-Free*

1 cup your favorite fruits (such as berries, banana, mango, pineapple, or a combination of fruit)

½ cup yogurt (plain, Greek, or flavored)

½ cup milk (dairy or plant-based)

1 tablespoon honey or maple syrup (optional, for added sweetness)

½ cup ice cubes (optional, for a chilled smoothie)

Wash and prepare your fruits by removing any peels, stems, or seeds. Chop larger fruits into smaller pieces for easier blending.

In a blender, combine the fruits, yogurt, milk, and sweetener (if using). If you prefer a thicker frozen smoothie, add the optional ice cubes.

Blend the ingredients on high speed until smooth and creamy. If the mixture is too thick, add a little more milk to reach the desired consistency.

Taste the smoothie and adjust the sweetness by adding more honey or maple syrup if desired. Blend again to incorporate the additional sweetener.

Pour the fruit smoothie into glasses or jars.

Serve immediately.

NOTE

Experiment with different fruits, add a handful of spinach or kale for extra greens, or include a scoop of protein powder for a boost of protein. Feel free to adjust the quantities of the ingredients to suit your taste and desired thickness.

Trivia

How many characters have their tonsils removed over the eleven seasons of the show?

Hot Chocolate
with Tiny Marshmallows

Living through cold Wisconsin winters—even fake ones—required a bracing drink. That's right, when Fonz needed a warming pick-me-up, his favorite was the hot sweetness of Hot Chocolate. The Tiny Marshmallows are essential, but Fonzie wouldn't judge if you use store-bought.

Hot Chocolate

PREP TIME: *10 minutes* | **COOK TIME:** *7 to 10 minutes* | **YIELD:** *two 8-ounce servings* | **DIETARY NOTE:** *Vegetarian, Gluten-Free*

2 cups milk (can substitute plant-based milk)

2 tablespoons unsweetened cocoa powder

2 tablespoons granulated sugar

Pinch of salt

¼ teaspoon 100% pure vanilla extract

Top with Tiny Marshmallows

In a small saucepan, heat milk over medium heat until it starts to steam. Do not let it boil.

In a separate bowl, whisk together the cocoa powder and sugar and salt, to taste, until well combined.

Gradually whisk the cocoa mixture into the hot milk, stirring continuously to dissolve any lumps.

Continue to cook the mixture over medium heat, stirring constantly, until it reaches your desired temperature and consistency, about 3 to 5 minutes.

Remove the saucepan from heat and stir in the vanilla extract.

Pour the hot cocoa into mugs and top with Tiny Marshmallows. Serve immediately.

NOTE

Feel free to adjust the sweetness of the hot cocoa by adding more or less sugar according to your taste. You can also customize your hot cocoa by adding a pinch of cinnamon or a dash of peppermint extract for extra flavor.

Trivia

Fonzie had a recurring nemesis who refused to see the real Fonz but judged him by his leather jacket. Who was it?

Tiny Marshmallows

PREP TIME: *40 minutes active* | **CHILL TIME:** *24 hours* | **COOK TIME:** *12 to 14 minutes*
YIELD: *depends on final cut size, as few as 12 large pieces or up to 60 tiny pieces* | **DIETARY NOTE:** *Gluten-Free*

1 cup cold water, divided

3 envelopes unflavored gelatin (about 2½ tablespoons)

2 cups granulated sugar

¼ teaspoon salt

2 teaspoons 100% pure vanilla extract

Powdered sugar, for dusting

In the bowl of a stand mixer, pour ½ cup of cold water and sprinkle the gelatin over it. Let it sit for about 10 minutes to soften and bloom.

In a saucepan, combine the granulated sugar, ½ cup of cold water, and salt. Place the saucepan over medium heat and stir until the sugar dissolves completely.

Increase the heat to high and bring the sugar mixture to a boil. Insert a candy thermometer into the saucepan and continue boiling until the mixture reaches soft-ball stage or 240°F. When the sugar mixture reaches the soft-ball stage, remove the saucepan from heat.

With the stand mixer running on low speed, slowly pour the hot sugar syrup into the gelatin mixture in a steady stream. When all the syrup has been added, increase the mixer speed to high and continue to whip the mixture for about 10 to 12 minutes, or until it becomes thick and fluffy.

During the last minute of whipping, add the vanilla extract and mix until well combined.

Prepare a 9-by-13-inch baking dish by lightly greasing it and dusting it with powdered sugar.

Pour the whipped marshmallow mixture into the prepared baking dish, smoothing the top with a spatula.

Let the marshmallows set at room temperature for 24 hours, until they become firm and springy.

When the marshmallows are set, dust a clean surface with powdered sugar. Carefully invert the baking dish onto the surface, releasing the marshmallow block. Dust a sharp knife with powdered sugar to prevent sticking and cut the marshmallows into cubes.

Toss the cut marshmallows in additional powdered sugar to prevent sticking and store them in an airtight container at room temperature.

Potsie's "Ketchup" Freeze

Too broke to buy a soda from Arnold's? Potsie has the perfect solution—ketchup mixed into an ice-filled glass. Do you dare? Try this version of Potsie's Ketchup Freeze, with raspberries instead of tomatoes. Much better.

PREP TIME: *15 minutes* | **COOK TIME:** *5 minutes* | **CHILL TIME:** *60 minutes*
YIELD: *about 8 ounces of "ketchup" to make 8 freezes* | **DIETARY NOTE:** *Vegetarian, Vegan, Gluten-Free*

2 cups fresh raspberries

¼ cup granulated sugar

1 tablespoon fresh lemon juice

½ teaspoon vanilla extract

Ice cubes

NOTE

"Ketchup" can also be frozen for longer storage. Pour it into ice cube trays or freezer-safe containers and freeze until solid. Thaw in the refrigerator before using to make Freezes.

Rinse the fresh raspberries under cold water and pat them dry with a paper towel.

In a small saucepan, combine the raspberries, granulated sugar, and fresh lemon juice. Stir gently to coat the raspberries with the sugar.

Place the saucepan over medium heat and bring the mixture to a simmer. Reduce the heat to low and continue cooking for about 3 to 5 minutes, or until the raspberries have softened and released their juices. Remove the saucepan from the heat and let the mixture cool slightly.

Pour the raspberry mixture into a blender or food processor. Add the vanilla extract.

Blend the mixture on high speed until smooth and well combined. (Or strain the mixture through a fine-mesh sieve to remove the seeds for a smoother texture.)

Transfer the raspberry coulis to a container or jar with a tight-fitting lid if not using full amount immediately. Allow it to cool completely before making Freeze or storing.

Place the container of raspberry "Ketchup" in the refrigerator and chill for at least 1 hour.

Store any leftover "Ketchup" in a sealed container in the refrigerator for up to 5 days.

TO MAKE THE KETCHUP FREEZE:
Fill blender with 2 cups of ice cubes. Add about 1 ounce of "ketchup." Blend at high speed until fully integrated.

Pour into glasses and drink with a straw.

Arnold's Cherry Limeade

Paula Petralunga might have requested a custom Cherry Limeade from Arnold's after watching the submarine races at Inspiration Point with Fonzie. And Fonzie the gentleman that he was would have asked Al to make it for her. It's sweet and sour and refreshing and perfect for cooling off when you're feeling, um, overheated.

PREP TIME: *30 minutes* | **COOK TIME:** *about 15 minutes* | **YIELD:** *3 to 4 pints of concentrate* | **DIETARY NOTE:** *Vegetarian, Vegan, Gluten-Free*

3 cups cherries, stemmed and pitted (can substitute frozen cherries)

2 cups freshly squeezed lime juice (can substitute with bottled lime juice)

3 cups sugar

Trivia

Paula Petralunga appears and is mentioned in the first four seasons then not again until season ten. What happened to Paula?

TO MAKE THE CONCENTRATE:

Use a food processor or blender to puree cherries in batches until smooth.

Transfer the cherry puree to a non-reactive saucepan over medium-high heat until puree is warmed, about 5 minutes. Add the lime juice and sugar, stirring well to combine.

Continue cooking until sugar is fully dissolved. Remove from heat just before mixture comes to a boil. Cool.

Store in jars that can be refrigerated or in freezer-safe containers for longer storage in freezer.

TO MAKE THE CHERRY LIMEADE:

Mix one part concentrate with one part water, seltzer water, or ginger ale. Adjust the amount of concentrate to suit your taste preferences.

K.C.'s Strawberry Basil Iced Tea

A glass of this fruity, sweet Southern-style iced tea gives cousin K.C. the courage to face her first date at Arnold's Halloween dance with Melvin Belvin, who's more nervous than she is. Don't worry, K.C., Uncle Howard will teach you to drive soon no matter how much he dreads it.

PREP TIME: *15 minutes* | **COOK TIME:** *5 to 7 minutes* | **CHILL TIME:** *60 minutes*
YIELD: *six to seven 8-ounce servings* | **DIETARY NOTE:** *Vegetarian, Gluten-Free*

6 cups water

4 black tea bags

1 cup fresh strawberries, hulled and sliced

¼ cup fresh basil leaves, torn

¼ cup honey or sweetener of choice

Ice cubes

Fresh strawberries and basil leaves for garnish (optional)

In a large saucepan, bring 6 cups of water to a boil.

Once the water reaches a rolling boil, remove it from heat and add the black tea bags. Let the tea steep for 5 to 7 minutes to infuse the flavors. Remove the tea bags and discard them.

Add the sliced strawberries and torn basil leaves to the hot tea. Stir gently to combine.

Let the tea mixture cool to room temperature to allow the flavors to meld.

Once the tea has cooled, strain it through a fine-mesh sieve to remove the strawberry and basil solids. Compost the solids.

Stir in honey or your choice of sweetener until it dissolves completely. Adjust the sweetness to your liking.

Transfer the strawberry basil tea to a pitcher and refrigerate for at least 1 hour to chill.

When ready to serve, fill glasses with ice cubes and pour the chilled strawberry basil tea over the ice. Garnish each glass with a fresh strawberry and a sprig of basil, if desired.

Trivia

Why did K.C. Cunningham move to Milwaukee to live with the Cunningham's?

Side Dishes and Vegetables

Mrs. Cunningham knows rambunctious teenagers like Joanie and Ritchie can't live on burgers and fries. They need vegetables, roughage, vitamins, and, you know—healthy foods. Here are favorites with great flavors and little surprises to guarantee that even Fonzie eats his veggies.

Curried Pan-Fried Carrots

Mr. Cunningham has fond memories of succotash from his army days, but if you're like Joanie and succotash makes you sick, try these easy curried carrots—they're healthy and delicious.

PREP TIME: *15 minutes* | **COOK TIME:** *20 to 25 minutes* | **YIELD:** *4 to 6 servings* | **DIETARY NOTE:** *Vegetarian, Gluten-Free*

2 tablespoons olive oil

2 teaspoons curry powder

1 teaspoon ground cumin

½ teaspoon ground turmeric

½ teaspoon paprika

½ teaspoon salt

¼ teaspoon ground black pepper

1½ pounds carrots, peeled and cut into 4-to-6-inch-long sticks

Fresh cilantro or parsley, for garnish (optional)

Preheat oven to 425°F and line a sheet pan with parchment paper.

In a large bowl, combine the olive oil, curry powder, ground cumin, ground turmeric, paprika, salt, and black pepper. Stir well to create a smooth curry spice mixture.

Add the carrot sticks to the bowl with the curry spice mixture. Toss the carrots until they are evenly coated with the spices.

Transfer the spiced carrots to the prepared sheet pan, spreading them out in a single layer.

Place the sheet pan in the oven and roast the carrots for 20 to 25 minutes, or until they are tender and slightly caramelized. Flip the carrot sticks halfway through the cooking time to ensure even browning.

Remove the sheet pan from the oven and let the fried curried carrots cool for a few minutes.

Garnish the carrots with fresh cilantro or parsley, if desired.

 PAIRS WELL WITH Mrs. C.'s Meatloaf (page 111), Oven-Broasted Chicken (page 133), or TV Dinner Salisbury Steak (page 119).

Mr. C.'s "Feed the Platoon" Candied Yams

Sgt. Howard "Cookie" Cunningham reigned over the mess hall during his Army days. All the soldiers waiting to be sent to fight loved this delicious reminder of home. This recipe is scaled to feed a family (not army) platoon.

PREP TIME: *20 minutes* | **COOK TIME:** *45 to 50 minutes* | **YIELD:** *6 servings* | **DIETARY NOTE:** *Vegetarian, Gluten-Free*

4 medium-sized yams (1½ to 2 pounds)

½ cup (1 stick) unsalted butter

1 cup packed brown sugar

¼ cup pure maple syrup

1 teaspoon 100% pure vanilla extract

½ teaspoon ground cinnamon

¼ teaspoon ground nutmeg

¼ teaspoon kosher salt

1 cup pecan halves (for topping)

NOTE

Feel free to adjust the sweetness of the candied yams by adding more or less brown sugar and maple syrup according to your taste preference.

Preheat oven to 375°F. Grease a 9-by-13-inch baking dish with butter or cooking spray.

Peel the yams and cut them into ½-inch-thick slices. Arrange the slices in a single layer in the greased baking dish.

In a small saucepan, melt the butter over medium heat. Add the brown sugar, maple syrup, vanilla extract, ground cinnamon, ground nutmeg, and salt. Stir until the sugar is dissolved and the mixture is well combined.

Pour the buttery sugar mixture over the sliced yams, ensuring all the slices are coated evenly.

Cover the baking dish with aluminum foil and place in the oven and bake for 30 minutes.

Remove the foil and baste the yams with the syrup from the bottom of the dish. Continue baking, uncovered, for an additional 15 to 20 minutes or until the yams are tender and caramelized.

In a small skillet over medium heat, toast the pecan halves until fragrant and slightly browned. This will take about 3 to 5 minutes. Keep a close eye on them to prevent burning.

Remove the candied yams from the oven and let them cool for a few minutes. Serve them warm, topped with toasted pecans.

PAIRS WELL WITH Oven-Broasted Chicken (page 133), Mrs. C.'s Meatloaf (page 111), and Sunday Baked Ham (page 120).

Food Fight Rolls *with* Herb Butter

Who throws these delicious rolls at the Grand Poobah? When the Leopard Lodge meets all bets are off, so watch out for the hidden whoopie cushions. But please, for Mrs. C.'s sake, save the food fights for the Leopard Convention.

PREP TIME: *45 minutes active* | **CHILL TIME:** *2½ hours total* | **COOK TIME:** *25 to 35 minutes*
YIELD: *12 to 16 rolls* | **DIETARY NOTE:** *Vegetarian*

1 envelope active dry yeast

¼ cup warm water (110°F to 115°F)

1 cup whole milk

¼ cup vegetable shortening

3 tablespoons sugar

1½ teaspoons kosher salt

1 room-temperature egg

3½ cups all-purpose flour

¼ cup unsalted butter

Flaky sea salt for topping

FOR THE HERB BUTTER:

1 cup unsalted butter, softened

2 tablespoons fresh herbs (such as parsley, thyme, rosemary, or a combination), finely chopped

1 teaspoon lemon juice

½ teaspoon salt

¼ teaspoon ground black pepper

In a small bowl, whisk together 1 envelope of active dry yeast and ¼ cup warm water. Let it stand for 5 minutes.

Heat the whole milk in a small saucepan over medium heat until it is just warm. Remove from heat and set aside.

In a large bowl, combine the vegetable shortening, sugar, and kosher salt. Add the warm milk to the bowl and whisk to blend, breaking up the shortening into small clumps (it may not melt completely). Whisk in the yeast mixture and the room-temperature egg.

Add the all-purpose flour to the bowl and stir vigorously with a wooden spoon until the dough forms. Knead the dough with lightly floured hands on a lightly floured surface until it becomes smooth, which should take about 4 to 5 minutes.

Transfer the dough to a lightly oiled bowl, turning the dough a few times to coat. Loosely cover the bowl with plastic wrap. Let the dough stand at room temperature until it doubles in size, which usually takes about 90 minutes.

Preheat the oven to 350°F. Melt ¼ cup of unsalted butter in a microwave.

Lightly brush a 13-by-9-inch baking dish with some melted butter.

Punch down the dough in the bowl and divide it into 4 equal pieces.

Working with one quarter section at a time, roll dough out on a lightly floured surface into a 12-by-6-inch rectangle.

Cut the rectangle lengthwise into three 2-inch-wide strips. Cut each 2-inch strip crosswise into three 4-by-2-inch rectangles. Brush half of each 4-by-2-inch rectangle (covering about 2-by-2 inches) with melted butter. Fold the unbuttered side over, allowing a ¼-inch overhang. Place the folded rectangle flat in one corner of the baking dish, with the folded edge against the short side of the dish.

Add the remaining prepared dough pieces, shingling them to form one long row. Repeat the process with the remaining dough to create 4 rows of rolls. Brush the rolls with melted butter, loosely cover them with plastic wrap, and chill in the refrigerator for 60 minutes.

Bake the rolls until they turn golden and puff up, which should take about 25 to 35 minutes. Remove from the oven and brush the baked rolls with butter. Sprinkle flaky sea salt over the rolls.

Serve warm with Herb Butter.

Recipe continues on next page

TO MAKE THE HERB BUTTER:

In a bowl, add the softened butter. Add the finely chopped fresh herbs to the bowl. You can use a single herb or a combination of your choice, such as parsley, thyme, rosemary, or a mix.

Squeeze in the lemon juice to enhance the flavor of the herb butter. Sprinkle in salt and black pepper for seasoning. Mix all the ingredients together thoroughly until well combined.

Place the herb butter onto a sheet of parchment or wax paper. Shape the butter into a log or a desired form by rolling it in the paper. Twist the ends of the paper to secure the shape.

Refrigerate the herb butter for at least 1 hour, or until firm. Once chilled and firm, the herb butter is ready to be used.

Store any unused herb butter in an airtight container in the refrigerator for up to 2 weeks or freeze it for longer storage.

Trivia

Aside from Ron Howard's dad, Rance, what other Howard family members appeared on the show?

Cranberry Sauce

Marion long ago decided that Cranberry Sauce is much too delicious to only serve on Thanksgiving. She makes it for all her turkey and chicken dishes. Sweet, tart, and tangy; spread a spoonful on your next turkey sandwich and have Thanksgiving every day.

PREP TIME: *10 minutes* | **COOK TIME:** *15 to 22 minutes* | **CHILL TIME:** *2 hours*
YIELD: *about 8 ounces* | **DIETARY NOTE:** *Vegetarian, Vegan, Gluten-Free*

½ cup sugar

⅛ cup water

1½ teaspoons red wine vinegar

1¼ cups fresh or frozen cranberries

¼ cup port wine

1 cinnamon stick about 3 inches long

In a medium saucepan, combine the sugar, water, and red wine vinegar. Bring the mixture to a boil over medium heat, stirring until the sugar is completely dissolved.

Add the cranberries to the saucepan and continue to boil until the cranberries start to pop. This will take about 5 to 7 minutes. Stir occasionally during the cooking process.

Pour in the port wine and add the cinnamon sticks to the saucepan. Stir well to combine all the ingredients. Reduce the heat to low and simmer the mixture for an additional 10 to 15 minutes, or until the sauce thickens to your desired consistency. Stir occasionally to prevent sticking or burning.

Remove the saucepan from the heat and let the cranberry sauce cool to room temperature.

Transfer the cranberry sauce to a glass jar. Seal the jar and refrigerate for at least 2 hours, or until the sauce sets and flavors meld together. Before serving, remove the cinnamon sticks and discard.

NOTE

This cranberry sauce can be made in advance and stored in the refrigerator for up to 2 weeks. The flavors will continue to develop over time. Before serving, remove the cinnamon sticks and discard. Enjoy the sweet and tangy flavor of this cranberry sauce with a hint of spirit.

 PAIRS WELL WITH Wine-Soaked Roast Turkey and Gravy (page 123) and Delux B.L.T. (page 49).

Trivia

In season six, Marion tells the story of the first Thanksgiving because she is frustrated that no one is helping her prepare the feast. What is everyone doing?

Kelp Family Chestnut Stuffing

Marion's mom had a sharp tongue, but all was forgiven when she finally passed along the secret Kelp family stuffing recipe to Marion. Trust her recipes, but don't listen to her advice—you will not go blind if you kiss a boy.

PREP TIME: *30 minutes* | **CHILL TIME:** *40 to 45 minutes* | **YIELD:** *8 servings* | **DIETARY NOTE:** *Vegetarian*

½ cup unsalted butter

1 large onion, finely chopped

2 celery stalks, finely chopped

2 garlic cloves, minced

1 teaspoon dried thyme

1 teaspoon dried sage

1 teaspoon dried rosemary, crushed

½ teaspoon salt

¼ teaspoon ground black pepper

1 cup packaged cooked chestnuts, roughly chopped

8 cups day-old bread cubes (white or whole-wheat)

2 cups chicken or vegetable broth

¼ cup chopped fresh parsley

Preheat oven to 350°F. Grease a 9-by-13-inch baking dish with butter.

In a large skillet, melt the butter over medium heat. Add the chopped onion, celery, and minced garlic. Sauté until the vegetables are softened and slightly golden, about 5 to 7 minutes.

Add the thyme, sage, dried rosemary, salt, and black pepper to the skillet. Stir and cook for an additional 2 minutes to release the aromatic flavors.

Roughly chop the packaged cooked chestnuts and add them to the skillet. Cook for another 2 minutes, stirring to combine all the ingredients evenly.

In a large mixing bowl, place the bread cubes. Pour the vegetable and chestnut mixture over the bread cubes.

Slowly pour the chicken or vegetable broth over the bread mixture, gently tossing to moisten all the bread cubes. The stuffing should be moist but not overly wet. Add more broth if needed.

Stir in the chopped fresh parsley, ensuring it is well incorporated into the mixture.

Transfer the stuffing mixture to the greased baking dish, spreading it out evenly. Cover the dish with aluminum foil and bake in the oven for 25 minutes. Remove the foil and continue baking for an additional 15 to 20 minutes, or until the top is golden brown and crispy.

Remove from the oven and let the stuffing rest for a few minutes before serving.

NOTE

If using packaged cooked chestnuts, you can find them in the grocery store's nut or baking section. Make sure to follow the package instructions for any necessary preparation, such as thawing or heating, before chopping and adding them to the recipe.

Fresh-Buttered Sweet Peas

A few hours away from the Cunningham home is Lake Whitefish, situated in the northern forests past the rolling green hills dotted with farms. Marion asks anyone driving back from the Lake to bring her fresh sweet peas from her favorite farm stand. Get the flavor but skip the drive with fresh pea pods from your favorite farmers' market.

PREP TIME: *15 minutes* | **COOK TIME:** *5 to 7 minutes* | **YIELD:** *4 servings* | **DIETARY NOTE:** *Gluten-Free*

1½ pounds fresh sweet peas, shelled

3 tablespoons unsalted butter

¼ cup finely chopped shallots

2 garlic cloves, minced

1 teaspoon fresh thyme leaves

½ teaspoon salt

¼ teaspoon ground black pepper

1 tablespoon freshly squeezed lemon juice

2 tablespoons chopped fresh parsley, for garnish (optional)

Bring a large pot of salted water to a boil. Add the shelled peas and cook for 2 to 3 minutes until they are bright green and tender-crisp. Avoid overcooking to retain the vibrant color and texture. Drain the peas and set them aside.

In a large skillet, melt the butter over medium heat. Add the finely chopped shallots and minced garlic. Sauté for 2 to 3 minutes until the shallots are translucent and fragrant.

Add the cooked peas to the skillet. Sprinkle with fresh thyme leaves, salt, and black pepper. Toss gently to coat the peas with the butter and seasonings. Cook the peas for an additional 2 to 3 minutes, stirring occasionally, until they are heated through and well coated with the buttery mixture.

Remove the skillet from heat and drizzle the freshly squeezed lemon juice over the peas. Toss lightly to distribute the lemon juice evenly.

Transfer the buttered peas to a serving dish. Sprinkle with chopped fresh parsley, if desired.

 PAIRS WELL WITH Mr. C.'s Favorite Pot Roast (page 112), Joanie's Favorite Pork Chops and Applesauce (page 116), and TV Dinner Salisbury Steak (page 119).

NOTE

Adjust the seasoning according to your taste preference. Feel free to add a pinch of red pepper flakes for a touch of heat.

Trivia

What do Howard and Marion receive as a gift from Richie and Joanie for their 20th wedding anniversary?

Green Beans Almondine

Mrs. C. makes these for Fonzie because he secretly confessed that he loves vegetables. While burgers and fries are great, no man can live on Arnold's alone.

PREP TIME: *15 minutes* | **COOK TIME:** *10 to 14 minutes* | **YIELD:** *4 servings* | **DIETARY NOTE:** *Vegetarian, Gluten-Free*

1 pound green beans, ends trimmed

2 tablespoons unsalted butter

½ cup slivered almonds

1 garlic clove, minced

1 tablespoon lemon juice

Pinch of salt

Pinch of ground black pepper

Bring a large pot of salted water to a boil. Add the green beans and cook for about 4 to 5 minutes, or until they are crisp-tender. Drain the beans and set aside.

In a large skillet, melt the butter over medium heat. Add the slivered almonds and cook, stirring occasionally, until they are golden brown and fragrant. This should take about 3 to 4 minutes.

Add the minced garlic to the skillet and sauté for about 1 minute, until it becomes aromatic.

Add the cooked green beans to the skillet and toss them with the almond and garlic mixture until well coated. Cook for an additional 2 to 3 minutes, allowing the flavors to meld.

Drizzle the lemon juice over the green beans and season with salt and ground black pepper to taste. Toss everything together to evenly distribute the seasoning.

Transfer the Green Bean Almondine to a serving dish and garnish with additional slivered almonds.

Trivia

Marion Cunningham was a proud homemaker first and foremost, but she did attend college. What did she major in?

PAIRS WELL WITH Chicken Cordon Bleu à la Chez Antoine (page 140), Sunday Baked Ham (page 120), and Al's Fish Fry with Tartar Sauce (page 136).

Mushroom Wild Rice

Fonzie always thought he was an only child . . . but not so fast! Turns out his no-good father Vito had another son named Arthur who is nothing like Fonzie. The other Arthur, who goes by Artie, is a vegetarian from San Francisco, whoa! Serve this as an entrée to Artie and a side dish for Fonz.

PREP TIME: *20 minutes* | **COOK TIME:** *60 to 75 minutes* | **YIELD:** *4 servings* | **DIETARY NOTE:** *Vegetarian, Gluten-Free*

1 cup wild rice

2 cups vegetable broth

1 tablespoon unsalted butter

1 tablespoon olive oil

2 garlic cloves, minced

1 small onion, finely chopped

1 pound fresh mushrooms (such as cremini, portabella, or white), sliced

1 teaspoon fresh thyme leaves

½ teaspoon salt

¼ teaspoon ground black pepper

2 tablespoons chopped fresh parsley, for garnish (optional)

Rinse the wild rice thoroughly under cold water. In a medium saucepan, combine the rinsed wild rice and vegetable broth. Bring to a boil over medium-high heat.

Reduce the heat to low, cover, and simmer for 45 to 50 minutes, or until the rice is tender and the liquid is absorbed. Remove from heat and let it sit covered for 5 to 10 minutes.

In a large skillet, melt the butter and heat the olive oil over medium heat. Add the minced garlic and finely chopped onion. Sauté for 2 to 3 minutes until the onions are translucent and fragrant.

Add the sliced mushrooms to the skillet. Sprinkle with fresh thyme leaves, salt, and black pepper. Cook for 6 to 8 minutes, stirring occasionally, until the mushrooms are tender and lightly browned.

Add the cooked wild rice to the skillet with the mushrooms. Stir gently to combine and coat the rice with the mushroom mixture. Cook for an additional 2 to 3 minutes to heat through.

Remove the skillet from heat and transfer the mushrooms and wild rice to a serving dish. Sprinkle with chopped fresh parsley for added freshness and presentation.

PAIRS WELL WITH Oven-Broasted Chicken (page 133), Shrimp-and-Crab Stuffed Crepes à la Chez Antoine (page 143), and Chicken Cordon Bleu à la Chez Antoine (page 140), or as a vegetarian entrée.

Trivia

Artie sought out Fonzie to inform him that their father has indeed died and to give Fonz a special bequest from Vito. What is it?

Joanie's Baked Macaroni *and* Cheese

When your mom is the best cook on the block you have double favorites, like how Joanie loves Marion's Baked Macaroni *and* pork chops. But that doesn't mean she gets two weekly menu choices, that wouldn't be fair.

PREP TIME: *15 minutes* | **COOK TIME:** *25 to 30 minutes* | **YIELD:** *6 servings* | **DIETARY NOTE:** *Vegetarian*

8 ounces elbow macaroni

2 tablespoons unsalted butter

2 tablespoons all-purpose flour

2 cups milk

2 cups shredded cheddar cheese

½ teaspoon salt

¼ teaspoon ground black pepper

¼ teaspoon garlic powder

¼ teaspoon paprika

Preheat oven to 375°F.

Cook the elbow macaroni according to the package instructions until al dente. Drain the cooked macaroni and set it aside.

In a medium saucepan, melt the butter over medium heat. Add the flour to the melted butter and whisk continuously for about 1 minute to make a roux.

Gradually pour in the milk while whisking constantly to ensure a smooth mixture. Cook the sauce over medium heat, stirring frequently, until it thickens and comes to a gentle simmer. This usually takes about 5 minutes.

Remove the saucepan from the heat and stir in the shredded cheddar cheese until it melts, and the sauce becomes smooth. Add salt, black pepper, garlic powder, and paprika to the cheese sauce. Stir well to incorporate the seasonings.

In a large mixing bowl, combine the cooked macaroni and the cheese sauce. Stir until all the macaroni is coated with the sauce.

Transfer the macaroni and cheese mixture to a greased 9-by-9-inch baking dish or a similarly sized oven-safe dish. Place the baking dish in the oven and bake for 20 to 25 minutes, or until the cheese is bubbly and the top is golden brown.

Remove the baked macaroni and cheese from the oven and let it cool for a few minutes before serving.

Even Ralph Can Make Them Smashed Potatoes

If Ralph had used this recipe for smashed potatoes instead of his version of "mashies," he wouldn't have needed ten pots. Yet of the two, Ralph is a better cook than Potsie, who makes charcoal popsicles out of frozen TV dinners.

PREP TIME: *15 minutes* | **COOK TIME:** *35 to 40 minutes* | **YIELD:** *4 servings* | **DIETARY NOTE:** *Vegetarian, Gluten-Free*

1½ pounds baby red potatoes, scrubbed with blemishes removed

2 tablespoons olive oil

4 garlic cloves, minced

1 teaspoon dried rosemary

1 teaspoon dried thyme

½ teaspoon salt

¼ teaspoon ground black pepper

¼ cup grated Parmesan cheese (optional)

Chopped fresh parsley (optional)

NOTE

Smashed Potatoes are best enjoyed fresh from the oven when they are at their crispiest. However, they can be reheated in the oven briefly to regain some of their crunchiness if needed.

Trivia

The season five episode, "The Apartment," showed Potsie and Ralph moving into their new bachelor pad as a launch for another *Happy Days* spin-off show. The show never happened, but what other primetime *Happy Days* spin-off shows were broadcast?

Preheat oven to 425°F.

Place the potatoes in a large pot and cover them with cold water. Add a generous pinch of salt to the water. Bring the water to a boil over high heat. Reduce the heat to medium-low and simmer the potatoes for about 15 minutes, or until they are fork-tender.

While the potatoes are cooking, prepare a baking sheet by lining it with parchment paper or lightly greasing it with olive oil.

Drain the cooked potatoes and let cool for a few minutes until they are safe to handle.

Place the potatoes onto the prepared baking sheet, leaving space between each potato.

Using the bottom of a glass or a potato masher, gently press down on each potato to flatten it to about ½-inch thickness. Be careful not to break them apart completely.

In a small bowl, combine the olive oil, minced garlic, dried rosemary, dried thyme, salt, and black pepper. Stir well to combine. Brush or drizzle the seasoned oil mixture evenly over the smashed potatoes, making sure to coat each one.

Place the baking sheet into the oven and bake for about 20 to 25 minutes, or until they turn golden and crispy.

Remove the baking sheet from the oven and let the potatoes cool for a few minutes. If desired, sprinkle the smashed potatoes with grated Parmesan cheese and chopped fresh parsley for added flavor and garnish.

Dude Ranch Baked Barbeque Beans

Al perfected this recipe at Uncle Ben's dude ranch while everyone else worked to get ready for the big rodeo. Cowboys and city slickers both need lots of tasty protein when they're out ridin', ropin', and ranglin'.

PREP TIME: *15 minutes* | **COOK TIME:** *5 to 7 minutes* | **YIELD:** *about 8 servings*

Two 15-ounce cans navy beans, drained and rinsed

Two 15-ounce cans cannellini beans (white kidney beans), drained and rinsed

2 cups chopped onions

½ pound bacon, chopped

¼ cup cider vinegar

12 ounces canned tomato paste

1 cup molasses

2 tablespoons kosher salt

2 tablespoons honey (omit if using blackstrap molasses)

1 teaspoon Worcestershire sauce

1 teaspoon dry mustard

½ teaspoon cumin

2 teaspoons garlic, mashed

In a medium stock pot, combine the drained and rinsed canned beans, chopped onions, and bacon. Bring the mixture to a boil over medium heat, then reduce the heat to low. Cover the pot and simmer for 30 minutes, stirring occasionally.

Preheat oven to 325°F while the bean mixture is simmering.

Add the cider vinegar, canned tomato paste, molasses, kosher salt, honey, Worcestershire sauce, dry mustard, cumin, and mashed garlic to the simmering bean mixture. Stir well to combine while simmering, then remove from heat.

Transfer the bean mixture to a covered baking dish or Dutch oven. Cover the dish and bake for 2 hours. Uncover and bake for an additional 30 minutes.

Serve hot. Store leftovers in refrigerator when cooled. Mr. C. says that Dude Ranch Baked Barbeque Beans taste better the next day and makes them the day before the cookout.

 PAIRS WELL WITH Slow-Roasted Brisket (page 109), City Chicken (Mock Chicken Legs) (page 127), and Sunday Baked Ham (page 120).

 Trivia

Who played Marion Cunningham's Uncle Ben?

Leopard Lodge Oven-Roasted Corn on the Cob

There won't be any leftovers when the Leopard Lodge brings out the big grill for the Lodge's annual picnic. But you don't have to wait for the grill to make this oven roasted version anytime. Unlike one hundred pounds of Leopard Lodge Potato Salad (page 23).

PREP TIME: *15 minutes* | **CHILL TIME:** *60 minutes* | **COOK TIME:** *5 to 7 minutes* | **YIELD:** *4 servings* | **DIETARY NOTE:** *Vegetarian, Gluten-Free*

4 ears corn, husks removed

2 tablespoons olive oil

Salt

Ground black pepper

Butter, for serving (optional)

Fresh parsley or cilantro for garnish (optional)

Lime wedges, for serving (optional)

Preheat oven to 400°F.

Place the corn ears on a baking sheet or roasting pan. Drizzle the olive oil over the corn, ensuring all sides are coated. Sprinkle salt and ground black pepper over the corn, adjusting the amount according to your taste preferences.

Roast the corn for about 20 minutes, or until the kernels are tender and slightly charred. Flip the corn halfway through the cooking time to ensure even browning.

Remove the roasted corn from the oven and let it cool for a few minutes.

Serve the roasted corn on the cob with a pat of butter on top, allowing it to melt over the warm corn.

Garnish with fresh parsley or cilantro and a lime wedge, for added freshness and color.

Trivia

Howard Cunningham ascended from pledge master to Grand Poobah of the Leopard Lodge. But there was a rival fraternal organization in town that Lenny and Squiggy were members of. What was that group's name?

Pizza Bowl Air-Fried Mozzarella Sticks

The Ten Pins aren't the best bowling team in the league—Marion's average is only 119. Howard is better, but the real reason he joined the mixed league at the Pizza Bowl was to get his weekly treat of mozzarella sticks. Much healthier than fries, *right*?

PREP TIME: *15 minutes* | **COOK TIME:** *6 to 8 minutes* | **YIELD:** *24 pieces* | **DIETARY NOTE:** *Vegetarian*

12 mozzarella cheese snack sticks

½ cup all-purpose flour

2 large eggs, beaten

1 cup breadcrumbs

½ teaspoon dried oregano

½ teaspoon dried basil

½ teaspoon garlic powder

¼ teaspoon salt

=== NOTE ===

It's important not to overcrowd the air fryer basket to ensure proper air circulation and even cooking. You may need to fry the mozzarella sticks in batches depending on the size of your air fryer.

Trivia

Was there a real Pizza Bowl in Milwaukee?

Cut each mozzarella cheese stick in half, creating 24 shorter sticks. Set aside.

Preheat air fryer at 400°F for 5 minutes.

Place the flour in a shallow dish. In another dish, beat the eggs until well combined. In a third dish, combine the breadcrumbs, dried oregano, dried basil, garlic powder, and salt.

Take a mozzarella stick and coat it in the flour, shaking off any excess. Dip it into the beaten eggs, allowing any excess to drip off. Finally, roll the stick in the breadcrumb mixture, pressing gently to adhere. Place the coated stick on a baking sheet or wire rack. Repeat this process with the remaining mozzarella sticks.

Lightly spray the coated mozzarella sticks with vegetable oil spray to promote browning and crispiness.

Set your air fryer to 400°F. Place the mozzarella sticks in the air fryer basket, making sure they are in a single layer without overlapping. Cook the mozzarella sticks in the air fryer for 6 to 8 minutes, or until they turn golden brown and the cheese is melted and gooey.

Carefully remove the fried mozzarella sticks from the air fryer and let them cool for a minute or two.

Serve with marinara, pizza, or other sauce for dipping.

FROM **Arnold's** MENU

Arnold's makes the perfect side dishes . . . just be sure to eat them, not wear them!

FRENCH FRIES

Dip them in a chocolate Thick Milwaukee Malt (page 166). Split them three ways. Leave a trail of them if you've got to keep an eye on your little sister and Fonzie's cousin Spike. But if Mrs. Cunningham had her way, French fries would be taken off the menu because they cause bags under your eyes.

PREP TIME: *15 minutes* | **CHILL TIME:** *30 minutes* | **COOK TIME:** *20 minutes*
YIELD: *4 servings* | **DIETARY NOTE:** *Vegetarian, Vegan, Gluten-Free*

4 large Russet potatoes (about 2 pounds)

Vegetable oil spray

1 teaspoon sea salt

½ teaspoon garlic powder

½ teaspoon paprika

=== NOTE ===

These fries are best enjoyed fresh from the air fryer, as they may lose their crispiness upon cooling.

Trivia

While not exactly a cameo, who appears in the movie Richie, Carol, Spike, and Joanie are watching on their double date in season two?

Scrub the potatoes thoroughly under running water to remove any dirt. Pat them dry with a paper towel. Cut the potatoes into ¼-inch-thick sticks. Aim for uniformity in size to ensure even cooking.

Preheat air fryer at 400°F for 5 minutes.

In a large bowl, place the cut potatoes and fill it with cold water. Let the potatoes soak for 30 minutes. (This step helps remove excess starch, resulting in crispier fries.) Drain the potatoes and pat them dry with a clean kitchen towel or paper towels.

Lightly spray the air fryer basket with vegetable oil spray to prevent sticking. In batches, place the potatoes in the air fryer basket, ensuring they are in a single layer without overcrowding. Overcrowding will lead to uneven cooking.

Cook the fries in the air fryer for 15 minutes, shaking the basket halfway through to promote even browning. After 15 minutes, increase the temperature to 425°F and continue cooking for an additional 5 minutes to achieve a crispy exterior.

While the fries are cooking, combine the salt, garlic powder, and paprika in a small bowl.

Once the fries are done, carefully remove them from the air fryer basket and transfer them to a large bowl.

Immediately sprinkle the seasoning mixture over the hot fries, tossing gently to ensure even distribution.

ONION RINGS

We never learned if Arnold officially changed the menu after Richie declared live on the radio that the drive-in served "Richie the C" Onion Rings. Probably not though—Arnold was nearly as cheap as Mr. C. and wouldn't have wanted to spend money on a new menu sign.

PREP TIME: *30 minutes* | **COOK TIME:** *8 to 10 minutes* | **YIELD:** *4 servings* | **DIETARY NOTE:** *Vegetarian*

2 large yellow onions

1 cup all-purpose flour

1 teaspoon paprika

½ teaspoon garlic powder

½ teaspoon salt

¼ teaspoon ground black pepper

2 large eggs

1 cup panko breadcrumbs

Vegetable oil spray

=== NOTE ===

For optimal crispiness, it is recommended to serve the onion rings immediately after cooking. They may lose their crispiness upon cooling.

Trivia

Richie announces during the live remote broadcast at Arnold's that not only will Arnold's add "Richie the C" Onion Rings but another item. What was it?

Peel the onions and cut them into ½-inch-thick slices. Separate the rings and set them aside.

Preheat air fryer for 5 minutes.

In a shallow dish, combine the flour, paprika, garlic powder, salt, and black pepper. Mix well.

In a separate dish, beat the eggs until well combined.

Place the panko breadcrumbs in another shallow dish.

Take an onion ring and dip it into the flour mixture, ensuring it's evenly coated. Shake off any excess flour.

Dip the floured onion ring into the beaten eggs, allowing any excess to drip off.

Finally, coat the onion ring with panko breadcrumbs, pressing gently to adhere. Place the coated onion ring on a baking sheet or wire rack. Repeat this process with the remaining onion rings.

Lightly spray the coated onion rings with vegetable oil spray to promote browning and crispiness.

Working in batches, place the onion rings in the air fryer basket, making sure they are in a single layer without overlapping.

Cook the onion rings in the air fryer for 8 to 10 minutes, flipping them halfway through to ensure even browning.

Once the onion rings are golden brown and crispy, remove them from the air fryer and transfer them to a serving plate or place on baking sheet and in warm oven to hold until all onion rings are done. Repeat the frying process with the remaining onion rings until all are cooked.

Dinners

You can see the dining room table in your mind's eye. Joanie sets the table. Marion brings out one of these entrées. Oh, and Howard, Richie, and Fonzie will help clean up after Marion finally lets everyone know she's not their servant! Like every family, there were arguments and laughter and everyone around the table was among those they loved best.

Slow-Roasted Brisket

You don't have to be as cheap as Howard Cunningham to complain about beef prices. Slow roasting a cheaper cut of meat allows the flavor to develop and results in a tender and juicy brisket. While not as cheap as 68 cents a pound—the "high price" Howard complained about—it's still worth the cost!

PREP TIME: *1 hour* | **COOK TIME:** *15 to 20 hours* | **YIELD:** *6 to 8 servings*

3 tablespoons onion powder, divided

3 tablespoons garlic powder, divided

3 tablespoons mustard powder, divided

3 tablespoons ancho chile powder, divided

3 tablespoons light brown sugar, divided

2 teaspoons kosher salt

1 three-pound flat-cut brisket

1 cup ketchup

1 tablespoon Worcestershire sauce

1 teaspoon apple cider vinegar

=== NOTE ===

To create the aluminum foil "boat," take a large length of foil and carefully fold the ends toward the middle to form a boat shape. Unfold the foil to cover the brisket for the last phase of cooking.

Preheat the grill to 350°F. (If using a charcoal or wood-fired grill or oven, use an external thermometer to monitor temperature.)

In a small jar, thoroughly mix 2 tablespoons each of onion powder, garlic powder, mustard powder, ancho chile powder, and brown sugar, along with the kosher salt. This spice mix should yield about 1 full cup.

Trim the fat cap of the brisket so that there is a thin, even layer remaining.

Take half a cup of the spice mix and rub it evenly over the entire surface of the brisket. Let it sit at room temperature, uncovered, for 20 minutes.

Place the brisket fat-cap-side down over a direct flame on the grill and cook until the spices are browned, approximately 10 minutes. Flip the brisket and grill the other side for about another 10 minutes.

Adjust the grill heat to 250°F. Place the brisket on top of a large sheet of aluminum foil, creating a boat shape, and move it to a less hot area of the grill. Close the grill lid.

After 3 hours, insert an instant-read thermometer into the thickest part of the meat. When it reads 180°F, crimp the edges of the foil slightly to catch the juices from the meat as it finishes cooking.

Close the grill and continue cooking until the meat reaches 200°F, approximately 1½ to 2 hours.

Transfer the brisket to a cutting board and cover it with aluminum foil. Let it rest for 30 minutes.

In a medium microwave-safe bowl, combine the ketchup, Worcestershire sauce, remaining spice blend, and apple cider vinegar. Microwave the mixture until warm, about 1 minute. Collect any cooking juices and stir them into the sauce. Microwave again for another 1 minute.

Slice the brisket against the grain and serve it with the sauce.

 PAIRS WELL WITH Cunningham Coleslaw (page 26), Dude Ranch Baked Barbeque Beans (page 99), and Junior Chipmunk's Poke Cake (page 151).

Mrs. C.'s Meatloaf

Meatloaf. We're pretty sure you will love it too. Jefferson High School even served it for lunch. Mrs. C. lets the family pick one menu item for the week and Richie *always* picks meatloaf. You would—and now can—have Mrs. C.'s Meatloaf every night of the week. It's *fabamundo*!

PREP TIME: *20 minutes* | **COOK TIME:** *60 minutes* | **YIELD:** *6 to 8 servings*

½ cup breadcrumbs

½ cup milk

1½ pounds ground beef (80% lean, 20% fat)

½ cup finely chopped onion

2 garlic cloves, minced

¼ cup steak sauce (your preferred brand)

2 tablespoons ketchup plus ¼ cup for topping (optional)

1 tablespoon Dijon mustard

1 teaspoon salt

½ teaspoon ground black pepper

2 large eggs, beaten

Preheat oven to 375°F. Grease a loaf pan or line it with parchment paper for easy removal.

In a large mixing bowl, combine the breadcrumbs and milk. Let them sit for a few minutes until the breadcrumbs absorb the milk. Add the ground beef, chopped onion, minced garlic, steak sauce, ketchup, Dijon mustard, salt, black pepper, and beaten eggs to the bowl with the breadcrumb mixture.

Using your hands or a spoon, mix all the ingredients together until well combined. Be careful not to overmix, as this can make the meatloaf tough.

Transfer the mixture to the prepared loaf pan and shape it into a loaf shape. If desired, spread ¼ cup of ketchup over the top of the meatloaf for added flavor and moisture. Cover loaf pan with aluminum foil.

Place the loaf pan in the oven and bake for about 45 minutes. Remove aluminum foil and bake for 15 minutes more or until the meatloaf is cooked through and the internal temperature reaches 160°F.

Once cooked, remove the meatloaf from the oven and let it rest for a few minutes before slicing and serving.

Trivia

Fabamundo. Correctamundo. Perfectamundo. It was a classic Fonzie line but was never heard again after season five. Why?

Mr. C.'s Favorite Pot Roast

Marion knows the way to Howard's heart is definitely through his stomach. He would like her to make this pot roast every single weekend. It's the perfect lazy Sunday dinner but maybe not 52 times a year!

PREP TIME: *45 minutes* | **COOK TIME:** *5 to 6 hours* | **YIELD:** *6 to 8 servings*

1 cup sliced carrots

1 cup sliced yellow onions

1 cup chopped celery

1 cup sliced turnips

4 pounds chuck, round, or rump cut of beef

½ cup all-purpose flour

3 tablespoons butter (substitute with margarine if desired)

1 teaspoon kosher salt

1 teaspoon ground black pepper

1 teaspoon granulated garlic

1 bottle Shotz beer (or 12 ounces of your favorite lager-style beer)

Preheat oven to 350°F. Prepare the vegetables by washing, slicing, and chopping them as directed above. Set them aside for later use.

Remove the beef from its packaging. If the beef is in separate pieces, treat each piece individually. Trim away any silver skin or tough connective tissue.

Pour the flour onto a dinner plate. Roll each piece of beef in the flour until thoroughly coated. Set aside.

In a Dutch oven over medium heat, add the butter and allow it to melt, ensuring the bottom of the pan is coated. Place the floured beef into the Dutch oven and brown it on all sides. Pour the beer into the Dutch oven with the beef.

Cover the Dutch oven tightly and reduce the heat to low. Allow the pot roast to simmer for 4 hours, ensuring the beef becomes tender and flavorful.

After 4 hours, add the chopped vegetables and seasonings to the Dutch oven. Continue cooking for an additional 1 to 2 hours until the vegetables are tender, and the internal temperature of the beef is above 165°F. Remove from heat and allow to rest 20 minutes before serving.

Serve the pot roast with Even Ralph Can Make Them Smashed Potatoes (page 98) or boiled egg noodles. To make a delicious gravy from the cooking liquid, refer to the gravy recipe on page 123.

NOTE

If you have any leftovers, try making Mr. C.'s Weekend Hash with Poached Eggs (page 18) using the leftover pot roast.

"Cure-All" Chicken Soup *with* Dumplings

Richie got the flu and yes, bed rest, green gelatin, and French sunbathing films help him recover, but nothing cures like mom's chicken soup. Mrs. Cunningham's has fluffy floaty dumplings that absorb the flavorful broth that soothes and comforts.

PREP TIME: *20 minutes* | **COOK TIME:** *60 to 75 minutes* | **YIELD:** *4 to 6 servings*

1 tablespoon olive oil

1 onion, diced

2 carrots, diced

2 celery stalks, diced

3 garlic cloves, minced

2 to 3 cups shredded cooked chicken

6 cups chicken broth

1 bay leaf

1 teaspoon dried thyme

Pinch of salt

Pinch of ground black pepper

1 cup cake flour

2 teaspoons baking powder

½ teaspoon salt

1 egg

¾ cup milk

Fresh parsley, chopped (for garnish)

In a large pot, heat the olive oil over medium heat. Add the diced onion, carrots, celery, and minced garlic. Sauté until the vegetables become tender, about 5 minutes.

Add the shredded chicken to the pot. Stir and cook for another 2 minutes to warm up the chicken.

Pour in the chicken broth and add the bay leaf and dried thyme. Season with salt and pepper to taste. Bring the soup to a boil, then reduce the heat to low and simmer for about 20 minutes to allow the flavors to meld together.

While the soup is cooking, make dumpling dough.

Sift together the flour, baking powder, and salt into a medium-sized bowl. Set aside.

In a small bowl, crack egg and add milk. Beat well until fully blended. Slowly add the milk and egg mixture to the dry ingredients.

Gently mix with a fork or wooden spoon until ingredients are mixed but dough is still wet and sticky. Set aside.

Once the soup has simmered and the flavors have developed, remove the bay leaf from the pot.

Reduce heat to low simmer.

In batches, drop a teaspoon-size lump of dough into the soup pot. Repeat. Dumplings will expand during cooking and should not be crowded.

Replace the lid on pot and cook for 5 to 6 minutes. Remove lid and gently turn dumplings over. Replace lid and continue to cook for another 5 to 7 minutes.

When dumplings are fluffy and cooked, gently remove from pot with a slotted spoon and place 2 or 3 in a soup bowl. If more dough remains, repeat.

When all are cooked, ladle soup over dumplings, working to have an equal balance of broth, vegetables, and chicken. Garnish with freshly chopped parsley.

NOTE

Instead of shredded cooked chicken, you can use leftover Oven-Broasted Chicken (page 133) or grocery-store rotisserie chicken.

Trivia

What other food does Potsie and Ralph attempt to sneak to Richie while he's laid up with the flu?

Joanie's Favorite Pork Chops *and* Applesauce

Joanie loves pork chops and Mr. Cunningham hates them. Yet, whenever Mrs. C. makes Joanie's favorite dinner, Howard sets a good example and clears his plate. Another reason he keeps gaining and losing the same three pounds throughout season seven.

Pork Chops

PREP TIME: *15 minutes* | **CHILL TIME:** *15 minutes* | **COOK TIME:** *10 to 14 minutes* | **YIELD:** *4 servings* | **DIETARY NOTE:** *Gluten-Free*

4 bone-in pork chops, about 1 inch thick

1 teaspoon salt

½ teaspoon ground black pepper

½ teaspoon paprika

¼ teaspoon garlic powder

2 tablespoons vegetable oil

2 tablespoons unsalted butter

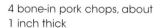

NOTE

Cooking times may vary depending on the thickness of the pork chops, so it's essential to use a meat thermometer to check for doneness. Remember to let the pork chops rest before serving to retain their juiciness.

Season the pork chops on both sides with salt, black pepper, paprika, and garlic powder. Let sit at room temperature for about 15 minutes to allow the flavors to meld.

Heat a large skillet or frying pan over medium-high heat. Add the vegetable oil and butter to the pan and let it melt.

Carefully place the seasoned pork chops in the hot pan. Cook for 4 to 5 minutes on the first side, until nicely browned. Flip the pork chops using tongs and cook for an additional 4 to 5 minutes on the other side. Adjust the cooking time depending on the thickness of the pork chops, ensuring they reach an internal temperature of 145°F for medium doneness.

Reduce the heat to medium-low and continue cooking for a few more minutes to ensure the pork chops are cooked through. Avoid overcooking to keep them juicy and tender.

Remove pork chops from pan and let them rest on a cutting board or plate for a few minutes to allow the juices to redistribute.

Applesauce

PREP TIME: *15 minutes* | **CHILL TIME:** *60 minutes* | **COOK TIME:** *20 to 25 minutes*
YIELD: *6 to 8 servings* | **DIETARY NOTE:** *Vegetarian, Vegan, Gluten-Free*

6 medium-sized apples (such as Granny Smith, Gala, or Fuji)

¼ cup water

2 tablespoons lemon juice

2 to 3 tablespoons granulated sugar

½ teaspoon ground cinnamon (optional)

NOTE

You can customize the applesauce by adding other spices like nutmeg or cloves, or even a touch of vanilla extract for extra flavor. Adjust the sweetness and texture based on your preference by adding more or less sugar and adjusting the level of mashing. Enjoy!

Peel, core, and roughly chop the apples into small pieces. Remove the seeds and tough parts of the core.

In a saucepan, combine the chopped apples, water, and lemon juice (if using). The lemon juice helps to enhance the flavor of the apples and prevents browning.

Place the saucepan over medium heat and bring the mixture to a simmer. Cover the pan and let it cook for about 15 to 20 minutes, stirring occasionally, until the apples are soft and tender.

Remove the saucepan from the heat and let the apple mixture cool slightly.

Using a potato masher, fork, or immersion blender, mash the cooked apples until you reach your desired consistency. If you prefer a smoother applesauce, you can use a blender or food processor.

Return the saucepan to low heat and stir in the granulated sugar and ground cinnamon (if desired). Adjust the sweetness and spice level according to your preference.

Cook the applesauce for an additional 5 minutes, stirring occasionally, to allow the flavors to meld together. Remove the applesauce from the heat and let it cool completely. The applesauce will thicken slightly as it cools.

When completely cooled, transfer the homemade applesauce to a jar or airtight container. Refrigerate for at least an hour before serving to allow the flavors to further develop.

TV Dinner Salisbury Steak

Chachi's devotion to Joanie extended to her cooking—nobody thaws a frozen TV dinner like she does! Here's a version of the classic that will inspire complimentary raves from the Chachi in your life.

PREP TIME: *30 minutes* | **COOK TIME:** *20 to 25 minutes* | **YIELD:** *4 to 6 servings*

- 1½ pounds ground beef (80% lean, 20% fat)
- ½ cup breadcrumbs
- ¼ cup finely chopped onion
- 2 garlic cloves, minced
- ¼ cup milk
- 2 tablespoons Worcestershire sauce
- 1 tablespoon Dijon mustard
- 1 teaspoon dried thyme
- 1 teaspoon dried parsley
- ½ teaspoon salt
- ¼ teaspoon ground black pepper
- 2 tablespoons butter
- 1 large onion, thinly sliced (about 1 cup)
- 8 ounces mushrooms, sliced
- 2 garlic cloves, minced
- 2 tablespoons all-purpose flour
- 2 cups beef broth
- 2 tablespoons Worcestershire sauce
- Pinch of salt
- Pinch of ground black pepper
- Chopped fresh parsley, for garnish (optional)

In a large mixing bowl, combine the ground beef, breadcrumbs, chopped onion, minced garlic, milk, Worcestershire sauce, Dijon mustard, dried thyme, dried parsley, salt, and black pepper. Mix well until all the ingredients are evenly incorporated.

Divide the mixture into 4 to 6 portions and shape each portion into an oval-shaped patty, about ½ to ¾ inch thick. Set aside.

Heat a large skillet over medium heat and melt the butter. Add the sliced onions and mushrooms to the skillet and sauté until they are golden brown and tender, stirring occasionally; about 5 to 7 minutes.

Stir in the minced garlic and cook for an additional minute until fragrant.

Push the onions and mushrooms to the side of the skillet and add the Salisbury steak patties to the center of the skillet. Cook the patties for about 4 to 5 minutes per side, or until they are browned and cooked through.

Remove the Salisbury steak patties from the skillet and set them aside on a plate.

Sprinkle the flour over the onions and mushrooms in the skillet, stirring well to coat them evenly. Cook for 1 to 2 minutes.

Slowly pour in the beef broth and Worcestershire sauce while stirring continuously. Continue to cook, stirring occasionally, until the gravy thickens and comes to a simmer for about 5 minutes.

Reduce the heat to low and return the Salisbury steak patties to the skillet, spooning some of the gravy over them. Simmer for an additional 5 minutes to allow the flavors to meld together. Season with salt and pepper to taste.

Serve the Salisbury steak patties with the mushroom and onion gravy, garnished with fresh parsley if desired.

NOTE

You can adjust the thickness of the gravy by adding more or less beef broth or by simmering it longer to reach your desired consistency.

Trivia

Joanie moved away from home to Chicago to do what?

Sunday Baked Ham

Sunday afternoons are for football and ham and rolls! It's a tradition that starts with making this succulent baked ham on the day before, resulting in an easy, eat-when-you're-hungry buffet of sandwich makings. It goes without saying that this Sunday Baked Ham is also a favorite holiday dinner centerpiece, but why wait for a holiday when there are fifty-two Sundays in a year!

PREP TIME: *30 minutes* | **COOK TIME:** *100 to 120 minutes* | **YIELD:** *8 to 10 servings* | **DIETARY NOTE:** *Gluten-Free*

1 fully cooked bone-in 7-to-8-pound ham

⅔ cup brown sugar

½ cup Dijon mustard

½ cup orange or pineapple juice

½ teaspoon garlic powder

One 15-ounce can pineapple rings (optional)

Whole cloves, for garnish (optional)

Trivia

Watching and attending football games is a recurring theme in *Happy Days*. Who is their favorite team?

Preheat oven to 325°F.

Remove any packaging or netting from the ham and place it in a large roasting pan, cut-side down.

Score the surface of the ham by making shallow diagonal cuts in a crisscross pattern. This will help the glaze penetrate the meat.

In a small bowl, mix the brown sugar, Dijon mustard, juice, and garlic powder to create the glaze.

Brush ¾ cup of the glaze over the surface of the ham, making sure to get into the scored cuts. Reserve ¼ cup of the glaze. If desired, place pineapple rings on surface of ham, secure with whole cloves.

Cover the roasting pan with foil and place in the oven.

Bake the ham for about 100 to 120 minutes or until the internal temperature reaches 140°F when measured with a meat thermometer. (Use the calculation of 15 to 20 minutes per pound of ham to adjust cook time as needed.)

Every 30 minutes, remove the foil and brush the ham with remaining glaze.

During the last 15 minutes of baking, remove the foil and increase the oven temperature to 375°F.

When the ham is fully cooked and has reached the desired internal temperature, remove it from the oven and let it rest for about 15 minutes before carving.

Slice the ham and serve it warm, drizzling any remaining glaze over the slices if desired.

PAIRS WELL WITH Even Ralph Can Make Them Smashed Potatoes (page 98), Curried Pan-Fried Carrots (page 83), or Fresh-Buttered Sweet Peas (page 91). Perfect for holiday celebrations or Sunday family dinners.

Wine-Soaked Roast Turkey *and* Gravy

When it's time for "The Talk," no daughter, or turkey for that matter, will wait. The correct ratio of wine to turkey is: one for the bird, one for the cook. How'd "The Talk" go? Well, Joanie would never have guessed her mom was at the dedication of Inspiration Point!

PREP TIME: *1 hour* | **COOK TIME:** *3 to 4 hours* | **YIELD:** *6 to 8 servings*

1 whole, 12-to-15-pound turkey

1 onion, quartered

1 whole celery, with 2 celery stalks cut into 4-to-6-inch-long pieces

3 pounds carrots, with 2 carrots peeled and cut into 4-to-6-inch-long pieces

4 to 6 garlic cloves, peeled

1 cup (2 sticks) unsalted butter, melted

1 tablespoon minced garlic

1 tablespoon kosher salt

2 teaspoons ground black pepper

1 bunch fresh rosemary

1 bunch fresh thyme

1 bunch fresh sage

1 bottle of white wine (can substitute with 2 cups chicken broth or turkey stock)

4 cups turkey or chicken broth

½ cup (1 stick) unsalted butter

½ cup all-purpose flour

½ cup whole milk

Pinch of kosher salt

Pinch of ground black pepper

Preheat oven to 325°F.

Remove the turkey from its packaging and remove the neck and giblets from the cavity (set them aside for other uses or discard).

Rinse the turkey inside and out with cold water and pat it dry with paper towels.

Place the turkey on a rack set inside a roasting pan. Lay a bed of onions, celery, and carrots on the bottom of the roasting pan and place turkey on top of the vegetables.

Stuff the turkey cavity with the quartered onion, celery chunks, carrot chunks, garlic cloves, and bundles of fresh herbs.

In a small bowl, combine the melted butter with the minced garlic, salt, and black pepper. With clean or gloved hands, carefully separate skin from meat on breast portion and carefully coat the meat with the butter mixture. Then brush the turkey with the butter mixture, making sure to cover all sides. Pour about 1 cup of wine (or broth) into the stuffed cavity and the remainder into the bottom of the roasting pan.

Cover the turkey loosely with aluminum foil, tucking it around the edges of the pan. Place the roasting pan into the oven. Bake for 1½ to 2 hours, then remove foil from the turkey and baste with pan drippings. (Save the foil.)

Continue to baste turkey every 30 minutes until fully cooked. (If not enough pan drippings, add an additional cup of wine, broth, or water to roasting pan.)

When close to calculated cooking time, insert a meat thermometer into the thickest part of the turkey's thigh, avoiding the bone. The turkey is done when the internal temperature reaches 165°F.

Once the turkey reaches the desired temperature, remove it from the oven, lightly cover with saved aluminum foil and let it rest for at least 20 to 30 minutes.

Carefully transfer the turkey to a serving platter or cutting board.

Pour the pan drippings (including any browned bits) into a measuring cup or bowl. Let the drippings sit for a few minutes to allow the fat to separate. Skim off the fat from the top of the drippings and reserve it for later use. If not enough pan drippings, add prepared chicken or turkey broth to bring total amount of liquid to 4 cups.

Recipe continues on next page

In a medium-sized saucepan, melt the unsalted butter over medium heat. Gradually whisk in the flour, stirring constantly to form roux. Continue to cook the roux for about 2 to 3 minutes until it turns a light golden color.

Slowly pour the reserved pan drippings and broth into the saucepan with the roux, whisking constantly to prevent lumps from forming. Add the milk, whisking until the mixture is smooth.

Bring the gravy to a gentle simmer and let it cook for about 5 to 10 minutes, stirring occasionally, until it thickens to your desired consistency. If the gravy becomes too thick, you can add more broth to thin it out.

Season the gravy with salt and pepper to taste. Continue to simmer the gravy for a few more minutes to allow the flavors to meld together.

Once the gravy reaches your desired thickness and flavor, remove it from the heat. (If your gravy has lumps, blend with immersion blender or strain through a sieve.)

Transfer the gravy to a serving bowl or gravy boat.

Carve the turkey into slices, starting with the breast and then moving to the thighs and drumsticks and serve with the gravy.

Trivia

What was the name of the fella who took Marion to Inspiration Point?

City Chicken (Mock Chicken Legs)

Mrs. Cunningham learned this recipe from her mother and cigar aficionado, Mrs. Kelp. Mother Kelp likes this recipe more than she likes her son-in-law, Howard, or as she calls him, "Fatso." But Howard gives as good as he gets, lamenting when her bursitis *isn't* causing her pain.

PREP TIME: *30 minutes* | **COOK TIME:** *60 minutes* | **YIELD:** *4 to 6 servings*

1 pound ground pork

1 pound ground veal (can substitute ground beef, 90% lean, 10% fat)

½ cup breadcrumbs

¼ cup milk

2 garlic cloves, minced

¼ cup finely chopped onion

¼ cup finely chopped fresh parsley

1 teaspoon dried thyme

1 teaspoon dried sage

½ teaspoon paprika

½ teaspoon kosher salt

¼ teaspoon freshly ground black pepper

4 wooden skewers, soaked in water for 30 minutes.

1 cup all-purpose flour

1 teaspoon paprika

½ teaspoon dried thyme

½ teaspoon dried sage

½ teaspoon garlic powder

½ teaspoon kosher salt

¼ teaspoon freshly ground black pepper

Vegetable oil, for frying

Preheat oven to 350°F.

In a large mixing bowl, combine the ground pork, ground veal, breadcrumbs, milk, minced garlic, chopped onion, parsley, dried thyme, dried sage, paprika, salt, and black pepper. Mix the ingredients thoroughly until well combined.

Divide the mixture into equal portions and shape each portion around a soaked wooden skewer, forming mock chicken legs. Make sure the meat is firmly packed around the skewers to maintain their shape during cooking.

In a shallow dish, combine the flour, paprika, dried thyme, dried sage, garlic powder, salt, and black pepper. Mix well.

Roll each mock chicken leg in the seasoned flour mixture, ensuring they are evenly coated on all sides. Set aside.

In a large skillet, heat vegetable oil over medium-high heat. Carefully place the coated mock chicken legs into the hot oil, a few at a time, without overcrowding the pan. Fry until golden brown on all sides, about 3 to 4 minutes per side. Transfer the browned mock chicken legs to a baking dish.

Once all the mock chicken legs are browned, place the baking dish in the oven and bake for 30 to 40 minutes or until the meat is fully cooked, reaching an internal temperature of 160°F.

Remove from the oven and allow the mock chicken legs to rest for a few minutes before serving.

Trivia

We hear about Mother Kelp throughout *Happy Days* and finally meet her in season eleven. Who played Mother Kelp?

"Swedish" Meatballs

There's no need to learn Swedish to make these party favorites. Marion tried to learn Swedish in hopes that Howard would take her to Sweden, but he'd rather save money and stay home. His cheapskate logic? Why spend when you can stay home and eat your way around the world.

PREP TIME: *20 minutes* | **COOK TIME:** *60 to 75 minutes* | **YIELD:** *4 servings*

1 pound lean ground beef (85% lean, 15% fat)

½ pound ground pork

½ cup breadcrumbs

¼ cup milk

¼ cup finely chopped onion

1 large egg

1 teaspoon salt

½ teaspoon ground black pepper

½ teaspoon garlic powder

¼ teaspoon allspice

¼ teaspoon nutmeg

2 tablespoons unsalted butter

1½ cups beef broth

½ cup grape jelly (reduce amount by half for less sweetness)

1 tablespoon Worcestershire sauce

2 tablespoons all-purpose flour

¼ cup heavy cream

Pinch of kosher salt

Pinch of ground black pepper

Chopped fresh parsley (optional)

In a large mixing bowl, combine the ground beef, ground pork, breadcrumbs, milk, chopped onion, egg, salt, black pepper, garlic powder, allspice, and nutmeg. Mix well until all the ingredients are evenly incorporated.

Shape the mixture into 1-inch meatballs and place them on a plate or baking sheet.

Preheat a skillet over medium heat and melt the butter. Working in batches, brown the meatballs on all sides until they develop a golden crust. Transfer the browned meatballs to the slow cooker.

In the same skillet, whisk together the beef broth, grape jelly, Worcestershire sauce, and flour. Cook over medium heat until the sauce thickens slightly and the grape jelly has melted.

Pour the sauce mixture over the meatballs in the slow cooker.

Cover the slow cooker and cook on high heat for 2 to 3 hours, until the meatballs are cooked through and tender.

Stir in the heavy cream and season with salt and pepper to taste. Continue cooking for an additional 15 to 20 minutes.

Serve the Swedish meatballs in a chafing dish for an hors d'oeuvres or buffet dinner, or over cooked egg noodles for a hearty dinner. Garnish with chopped fresh parsley, if desired.

Chachi's Mom's Spaghetti *and* Meatballs in Red Sauce

Have you ever sold your mom's leftover spaghetti and meatballs? Chachi did for two bucks a serving. Mrs. Arcola's spaghetti is that good. So good, in fact, that Louisa makes it for Al for a romantic dinner that results in their engagement.

Red Sauce

PREP TIME: *20 minutes* | **COOK TIME:** *120 to 135 minutes* | **YIELD:** *4 to 6 servings* | **DIETARY NOTE:** *Vegetarian, Vegan, Gluten-Free*

8 cups chopped paste tomatoes

1 tablespoon dried oregano

1 tablespoon dried parsley

1 tablespoon dried basil

1 tablespoon garlic powder

1 tablespoon onion powder

1½ teaspoons sugar (optional)

1½ teaspoons 100% pure sea salt

1½ teaspoons ground black pepper

2 tablespoons balsamic vinegar

2 tablespoons red wine

In a medium-sized stockpot, place the tomatoes. Over medium heat, cook the tomatoes until their skins begin to peel back and they release their juice, about 15 minutes.

When the tomatoes are softened, use an immersion blender to puree the tomatoes. (If there is no immersion blender, carefully and in batches, use a pitcher blender or food processor to puree.)

Add the remaining ingredients to the tomato puree and simmer over low heat for 2 hours. Stir occasionally to prevent scorching.

While the sauce is simmering, begin making the meatballs.

Preheat oven to 350°F. Line jelly roll pan with parchment.

Meatballs

PREP TIME: *30 minutes* | **COOK TIME:** *20 to 30 minutes* | **YIELD:** *about 16 meatballs*

1½ pounds ground beef (85% lean, 15% fat)

1 egg

½ cup minced white onion

3 tablespoons minced, fresh Italian parsley

1 teaspoon mashed garlic

½ teaspoon kosher sea salt

½ teaspoon ground black pepper

8 ounces Italian-flavored breadcrumbs

8 ounces grated Parmesan cheese

Olive oil

In a large bowl, combine the ground beef and egg using a fork. Set aside.

In a medium bowl, combine onion, parsley, garlic, salt, pepper, breadcrumbs, and cheese. Mix until evenly distributed.

Add the breadcrumb mixture to the ground beef mixture and mix with fork or gloved hands.

Shape the meatball mixture into balls approximately 3 inches in diameter, using gloved hands.

Recipe continues on next page

In a large frying pan, heat about 2 tablespoons of olive oil over medium-high heat. Place the meatballs in the hot frying pan and sear them, turning gently with a wooden spoon to sear on all sides.

Once seared, transfer the meatballs to the baking sheet and bake for about 20 minutes. When done, turn off heat and leave meatballs in warm oven.

While meatballs are baking and sauce is simmering, begin making the fresh pasta dough.

Fresh Pasta

PREP TIME: *20 minutes* | **CHILL TIME:** *30 minutes* | **COOK TIME:** *2 to 4 minutes* | **YIELD:** *4 servings* | **DIETARY NOTE:** *Vegetarian*

2 cups semolina or all-purpose flour

½ teaspoon salt

2 large eggs

½ cup water, as needed

NOTE

Substituting dried pasta for this recipe is just fine—but if you have the time, fresh pasta is always better! Fresh pasta cooks much quicker than dried pasta, so keep a close eye on it to avoid overcooking.

Trivia

Mrs. Louisa Arcola—Chachi's Mom—is played by what famous mom?

In a mixing bowl, combine the flour and salt. Make a well in the center.

Crack the eggs into the well and lightly beat them with a fork.

Gradually incorporate the flour into the eggs, mixing with a fork or your hands. If the dough seems dry, add water, a tablespoon at a time, until the dough comes together.

Once the dough forms a rough ball, transfer it to a clean, lightly floured surface. Knead the dough for about 5 to 7 minutes until it becomes smooth and elastic. If the dough feels sticky, sprinkle a little more flour as needed.

Shape the dough into a disk and wrap it tightly in plastic wrap. Let it rest at room temperature for at least 30 minutes to allow the gluten to relax.

After the resting period, unwrap the dough and divide into four smaller pieces. Take one portion and flatten it with your hands. Lightly flour the surface and roll out the dough using a rolling pin (or pasta machine). Roll the dough as thin as desired, keeping it in a rectangular shape.

Once rolled out, use a knife or pizza cutter to cut the pasta into fettuccine-sized (¼-inch-wide) strips.

Gently separate the cut pasta strands and lay them on a drying rack or clean towel to prevent sticking.

ASSEMBLING THE MEAL:

To cook the fresh pasta, bring a large pot of salted water to a boil. Add the pasta and cook for about 2 to 3 minutes, or until al dente. Cooking time may vary, so taste test to ensure the desired texture.

Drain the cooked pasta and place ½ to 1 cup into a pasta bowl. Ladle about ½ to 1 cup of red sauce over the pasta. Add 1 to 3 meatballs to the bowl. Garnish with shavings of fresh Parmesan cheese.

Oven-Broasted Chicken

The Leopard Lodge hosts Broasted Chicken one Saturday a month to raise money for their annual Poobah Doo Dah show. Al promised that his fifth cousin, Frankie Avalon, would perform at the 15th annual show. Boy, oh, boy, it's gonna be great. And this Oven-Broasted Chicken? It's gonna be great, too!

PREP TIME: *20 minutes* | **CHILL TIME:** *2 hours* | **COOK TIME:** *40 to 45 minutes* | **YIELD:** *4 to 6 servings*

2 cups buttermilk

1 tablespoon hot sauce (optional)

1 teaspoon salt

1 teaspoon paprika

½ teaspoon garlic powder

½ teaspoon onion powder

¼ teaspoon ground black pepper

2 cups all-purpose flour

2 teaspoons salt

2 teaspoons paprika

1 teaspoon garlic powder

1 teaspoon onion powder

½ teaspoon ground black pepper

4 to 6 chicken pieces (such as drumsticks, thighs, or bone-in breasts)

Cooking spray or vegetable oil

In a large mixing bowl, combine 2 cups of buttermilk, salt, paprika, garlic powder, onion powder, and black pepper.

Mix until thoroughly blended. Add the chicken pieces and toss to coat. Cover the bowl with plastic wrap and refrigerate for at least 2 hours or overnight.

Preheat oven to 425°F. Place a wire rack on a baking sheet and lightly grease it with cooking spray or brush it with vegetable oil.

In a separate bowl, combine the flour, salt, paprika, garlic powder, onion powder, and black pepper to make the coating mixture.

Remove the chicken pieces from the marinade and let any excess buttermilk drip off. Coat each piece of chicken thoroughly in the flour mixture, pressing the coating into the chicken to ensure even coverage.

Place the coated chicken pieces on the prepared wire rack on the baking sheet. Make sure to leave space between the pieces to allow for even cooking.

Lightly spray the top of the chicken pieces with cooking spray or drizzle them with a little vegetable oil. This will help the chicken become golden and crispy in the oven.

Bake the chicken in the oven for about 40 to 45 minutes, or until the chicken is cooked through and reaches an internal temperature of 165°F. The chicken should be golden brown and crispy. Remove the chicken from the oven and let it rest for a few minutes before serving.

Make a few extra pieces and use the leftovers in "Cure-All" Chicken Soup with Dumplings (page 115).

PAIRS WELL WITH Cunningham Coleslaw (page 26), Wedge Salad (page 27), or Green Beans Almondine (page 93).

═══ NOTE ═══

While this method does not replicate the exact pressure-fried results of a commercial broaster, it produces flavorful and crispy chicken with a similar texture.

Trivia

Frankie Avalon makes a guest appearance on the season nine "Poobah Doo Dah" episode. What song does he sing for the Doo Dah?

OUT TO EAT!

Even Marion Cunningham needed a break from cooking every now and then. Luckily there was Arnold's for everyone's favorite diner-style food and Chez Antoine for mid-century French-American-style cuisine. And it's always a treat when someone else is doing the dishes and cleaning the kitchen!

Arnold's Air-Fried Chicken Stand Tenders

You don't have to jump over twelve barrels on a motorcycle to enjoy this healthier version of Arnold's Fried Chicken. Serve it and have Arnold declare, "It's the biggest night in chicken history!"

PREP TIME: *30 minutes* | **COOK TIME:** *8 to 10 minutes* | **YIELD:** *about 4 servings*

- 1 pound boneless, skinless chicken breasts
- 1 cup all-purpose flour
- 2 teaspoons paprika
- 1 teaspoon garlic powder
- 1 teaspoon onion powder
- 1 teaspoon dried oregano
- ½ teaspoon salt
- ¼ teaspoon ground black pepper
- 2 large eggs, beaten
- 1 cup panko breadcrumbs

Preheat the air fryer to 400°F for about 5 minutes.

Slice the chicken breasts into long, thin strips, about 2 inches wide.

In a shallow dish, combine the flour, paprika, garlic powder, onion powder, dried oregano, salt, and black pepper. Mix well. In another shallow dish, place the beaten eggs. In a third shallow dish, spread out the breadcrumbs.

Take each chicken strip and coat it in the flour mixture, shaking off any excess. Dip it into the beaten eggs, allowing any excess to drip off. Finally, coat it in the breadcrumbs, pressing gently to adhere.

Place the coated chicken tenders on a plate or wire rack.

Lightly coat the air fryer basket with cooking spray or use an oil mister to lightly coat the chicken tenders.

Arrange the chicken tenders in a single layer in the air fryer basket, ensuring they do not overlap.

Cook the chicken tenders in the preheated air fryer for 8 to 10 minutes, flipping them halfway through, until they are golden brown and crispy.

Once the chicken tenders are cooked, remove them from the air fryer and let them cool for a few minutes.

Al's Fish Fry *with* Tartar Sauce

Kenosha's favorite son, Al Delvecchio, served up fish fry so good that his twin brother, Father Anthony, declared it "heavenly." Yep, yep, yep.

PREP TIME: *15 to 20 minutes* | **COOK TIME:** *10 to 12 minutes* | **YIELD:** *4 servings*

1 pound white fish fillets (such as cod, haddock, or tilapia)

1 cup all-purpose flour

1 teaspoon baking powder

½ teaspoon salt

¼ teaspoon ground black pepper

1 cup Shotz Beer (or other light lager or ale)

Vegetable oil, for frying

½ cup mayonnaise

2 tablespoons finely chopped dill pickles

1 tablespoon lemon juice

1 teaspoon Dijon mustard

1 teaspoon finely chopped fresh dill (optional)

Salt and ground black pepper

Pat the fish fillets dry with paper towels to remove any excess moisture. Cut the fillets into manageable-sized pieces, if needed.

In a mixing bowl, combine the flour, baking powder, salt, and black pepper. Whisk together to combine.

Slowly pour in the beer, whisking continuously, until the batter is smooth and well combined. The batter should have a thick but pourable consistency. If it is too thick, add a little more beer; if it is too thin, add a little more flour.

In a frying pan or skillet, pour enough vegetable oil to have a depth of about ½ inch. Heat the oil over medium-high heat until it reaches a temperature of 350°F.

Dip each piece of fish into the beer batter, coating it completely. Allow any excess batter to drip off before adding it to the hot oil.

Carefully place the battered fish pieces into the hot oil, making sure not to overcrowd the pan. Fry the fish for about 2 to 3 minutes per side, or until they are golden brown and crispy. Flip the fish halfway through the cooking time to ensure even browning.

Use a slotted spoon or tongs to remove the fried fish from the pan and transfer them to a paper towel–lined plate to drain excess oil. (Hold cooked pieces in warm oven if making multiple batches.)

In a small bowl, prepare the tartar sauce by combining the mayonnaise, finely chopped dill pickles, lemon juice, Dijon mustard, fresh dill (if using), salt, and pepper. Stir well to combine.

Serve the crispy beer-battered fish hot, alongside the tartar sauce for dipping.

=== NOTE ===

Adjust the seasoning of the tartar sauce according to your taste preferences. Feel free to experiment with different types of white fish for variety.

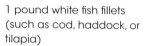

Trivia

Who played Father Anthony Delvecchio?

Pizza Bowl Sheet Pan Pizza

Laverne DeFazio's dad owned the best place to hang out—that wasn't Arnold's—the Pizza Bowl!
Grab this Sicilian-style loaded pie, a pitcher of Shotz, and pick up that split!

PREP TIME: *20 minutes* | **CHILL TIME:** *120 minutes* | **COOK TIME:** *60 to 75 minutes* | **YIELD:** *4 to 6 servings*

3½ cups all-purpose flour

2 teaspoons fine kosher salt

1 heaping teaspoon rapid or instant yeast (2 packages)

2 tablespoons extra virgin olive oil

1½ cups room-temperature water

OPTIONAL TOPPINGS:

8 to 12 ounces your favorite pizza sauce

½ pound bulk Italian sausage (If you can't find bulk sausage, use a link, and remove the casing. Approximately 4 links equal ½ pound.)

½ pound sliced pepperoni

1 pound shredded mozzarella cheese

½ cup shredded Parmesan cheese

8 ounces sliced mushrooms, canned

8 ounces sliced black olives

1 medium green pepper, chopped

1 medium onion, chopped

In the bowl of a stand mixer, combine the flour, salt, yeast, and 2 tablespoons olive oil. Whisk to combine.

Add water to the mixer and mix on medium speed until the dough comes together and no dry flour remains.

Increase the speed to medium-high and mix until the dough is stretchy and smooth, about 6 minutes. The dough should stick to the bottom of the bowl but pull away from the sides.

Pour the remaining olive oil into a rimmed baking sheet and spread it over the entire inner surface with your hands.

Transfer the dough to a 13-by-18-inch rimmed baking sheet and rub the top surface with oil until thoroughly coated.

Cover the baking sheet with plastic wrap and allow the dough to rise at room temperature until it has spread out to touch nearly each rim of the baking sheet, about 2 hours.

Thirty minutes before baking, adjust the oven rack to the middle position and preheat the oven to 550°F.

Carefully remove the plastic wrap from the pizza dough. Using oiled hands and being as gentle as possible to maintain air bubbles, push and stretch the dough into the corners of the pan by pressing out from the center and lifting each corner and stretching it beyond the edge of the pan. It should be pulled back until the pan is just filled with dough.

Top the pizza as desired with your favorite toppings.

Reduce the oven temperature to 500°F. Place pizza on the middle rack in the oven. Bake until the bottom is crisp, and the top surface is bubbling, about 15 to 20 minutes.

Allow the pizza to cool at room temperature for 5 minutes before serving.

NOTES

Any topping can be omitted or substituted to your personal taste. Make it vegetarian by omitting meats or substituting with plant-based Italian sausage and pepperoni.

To make the dough without a stand mixer, combine the flour, salt, yeast, and olive oil in a large bowl. Whisk to combine, then add water. Stir together vigorously with a wooden spoon until homogeneous, about 3 minutes. Cover the bowl with plastic wrap and allow it to rest at room temperature for at least 8 hours and up to 15. Continue with step 2 as directed.

Chicken Cordon Bleu *à la* Chez Antoine

Can chicken be intoxicating? Marion Cunningham thinks so after enjoying this dish at Chez Antoine. Howard thinks it may not be the food but the ample wine that accompanied dinner. Regardless of beverage, delight your senses with this simple and elegant dinner.

PREP TIME: *45 minutes* | **COOK TIME:** *18 to 25 minutes* | **YIELD:** *4 servings*

2 boneless, skinless chicken breasts

½ teaspoon salt

½ teaspoon ground black pepper

4 thin slices ham

4 thin slices Swiss cheese

½ cup all-purpose flour

½ cup breadcrumbs

2 large eggs, beaten

2 tablespoons vegetable oil

Trivia

It's 1962 and how much does a dinner for two at Chez Antoine cost?

Preheat oven to 375°F. Line a baking sheet with parchment paper.

Place the chicken breasts between two sheets of plastic wrap. Use a meat mallet or rolling pin to pound the chicken until it is about ¼ inch thick.

Season the chicken breasts with salt and pepper. Place a slice of ham and a slice of Swiss cheese on top of each chicken breast. Roll up the chicken, securing the filling inside. Use toothpicks to hold the rolls together.

Place the flour, breadcrumbs, and beaten eggs into three separate bowls.

Dip each chicken roll into the flour, coating it evenly. Shake off any excess flour. Then dip the chicken into the beaten eggs, allowing any excess to drip off. Finally, roll the chicken in the breadcrumbs, pressing gently to ensure the breadcrumbs stick.

Heat the vegetable oil in a large skillet over medium-high heat. Add the breaded chicken rolls and cook for about 2 to 3 minutes on each side, until golden brown. Remove the chicken from the skillet and place it on the prepared baking sheet.

Transfer the baking sheet to the oven and bake for 15 to 20 minutes, or until the chicken is cooked through and the cheese is melted.

Remove the toothpicks from the chicken rolls before serving. Slice the rolls into thick rounds and serve hot.

Shrimp-and-Crab Stuffed Crepes
à la Chez Antoine

Joanie is at Chez Antoine—but not with Chachi! It's one of Chachi's many rivals, Bill. Never fear: However crooked the path of true love, we know Joanie loves Chachi.

PREP TIME: *50 to 60 minutes* | **CHILL TIME:** *15 minutes* | **COOK TIME:** *25 to 30 minutes* | **YIELD:** *4 servings*

INGREDIENTS FOR THE CREPES:

- 1 cup all-purpose flour
- 1½ cups milk
- 2 large eggs
- 2 tablespoons melted butter
- ¼ teaspoon salt
- Cooking spray or additional butter for greasing the pan

INGREDIENTS FOR THE SHRIMP AND CRAB FILLING:

- 2 tablespoons butter
- 2 garlic cloves, minced
- ½ cup diced onion
- ½ cup diced bell pepper (any color)
- ½ pound shrimp, peeled and deveined
- ½ pound crab meat
- ½ cup diced tomato
- ½ teaspoon dried thyme
- ½ teaspoon paprika
- ¼ teaspoon red pepper flakes (optional, for heat)
- Pinch of salt
- Pinch of ground black pepper
- ¼ cup chopped fresh parsley
- Lemon wedges, for serving

TO MAKE THE CREPES:

Preheat oven to 250°F.

In a food processor or mixing bowl, combine the flour, milk, eggs, melted butter, and salt. Blend or whisk until smooth and well combined.

Let the batter rest for about 15 minutes to allow any bubbles to settle.

When the batter is ready, heat a nonstick skillet or crepe pan over medium heat. Lightly coat the surface with cooking spray or a small amount of butter.

Pour about ¼ cup of the crepe batter into the pan, tilting the pan in a circular motion to spread the batter evenly.

Cook the crepe for about 1 to 2 minutes, until the edges start to lightly brown and the center sets. Flip the crepe and cook for an additional 30 seconds to 1 minute.

Transfer the cooked crepe to an oven-safe plate and repeat the process with the remaining batter. Stack the crepes on the plate, separating each one with parchment paper or wax paper to prevent sticking. Place plate in warm oven to hold.

TO MAKE THE SHRIMP AND CRAB FILLING:

In a skillet over medium heat, melt the butter. Add the minced garlic, diced onion, and diced bell pepper. Sauté for about 3 to 4 minutes until the vegetables soften.

Add the shrimp to the skillet and cook for 2 to 3 minutes until they turn pink and opaque.

Stir in the crab meat, diced tomato, dried thyme, paprika, red pepper flakes (if using), and salt and pepper to taste. Cook for an additional 2 minutes to allow the flavors to meld together.

Remove the skillet from the heat and stir in the chopped fresh parsley.

TO ASSEMBLE THE CREPES:

Place a spoonful of the shrimp and crab filling on one side of each crepe.

Fold the crepe in half, enclosing the filling, and then fold it in half again to form a triangle or roll it up like an enchilada.

Serve the crepes warm with a squeeze of fresh lemon juice on top. Pairs well with Wedge Salad (page 27) or Pfister Salad (page 29).

Oysters Rockefeller *à la* Chez Antoine

Chez Antoine was the peak of sophistication where the French waiters (at least the ones who weren't faking the accent) showed the proper disdain for diners. The food was fantastic, but never ask for a doggy bag. In *Paree*, the dogs fend for themselves.

PREP TIME: *30 to 40 minutes* | **COOK TIME:** *60 to 75 minutes* | **YIELD:** *4 to 6 servings (2 to 3 oysters per person)*

12 fresh oysters, in the shell (see note for alternatives)

1 cup fresh spinach leaves, washed and stemmed

½ cup fresh parsley leaves, washed and stemmed

4 green onions, chopped

2 garlic cloves, minced

¼ cup (half stick) unsalted butter

¼ cup breadcrumbs

¼ cup grated Parmesan cheese

¼ teaspoon salt

¼ teaspoon ground black pepper

¼ teaspoon paprika

Lemon wedges, for serving

Preheat oven to 450°F. Line a baking sheet with aluminum foil.

Thoroughly scrub the oyster shells under cold water to remove any dirt or debris. Carefully shuck the oysters, ensuring the oyster liquor (juices) remains inside the shell. Set aside.

In a large pot of boiling water, blanch the spinach and parsley for about 1 to 2 minutes until wilted. Drain the greens and transfer them to a bowl of ice water to cool. Drain again and squeeze out any excess water.

In a food processor or blender, finely chop the blanched spinach and parsley, green onions, and garlic, without pureeing them.

Melt the butter in a skillet over medium heat. Add the chopped spinach mixture and sauté for about 3 to 4 minutes until the greens are cooked and any excess liquid has evaporated.

Stir in the breadcrumbs, Parmesan cheese, salt, black pepper, and paprika. Cook for another 1 to 2 minutes, stirring until the mixture is well combined and slightly toasted. Remove from heat.

Place the shucked oysters on the lined baking sheet. Generously spoon the spinach mixture onto each oyster, ensuring they are completely covered.

Place baking sheet in the oven and bake for about 10 to 12 minutes until the topping is lightly browned and the oysters are cooked through.

Remove from the oven and let cool for 1 to 2 minutes before serving. Serve on a platter or individual plates, garnished with lemon wedges.

Just before eating, squeeze fresh lemon juice over each oyster to enhance flavors.

=== **NOTE** ===

Oysters can be delicate, so handle them with care when shucking and during the cooking process. Frozen oysters can be substituted for fresh, however, it's important to thaw before attempting to shuck. And finally, you can use pre-shucked oysters in the recipe. Since the oysters are already shucked, you can skip the shucking step and proceed with the remaining instructions, starting from blanching the spinach and parsley. Spoon the spinach mixture onto each pre-shucked oyster and continue with the baking process as instructed.

Desserts

Who doesn't have a sweet tooth? Especially when Mrs. Cunningham is baking, Howard sneaks a piece of cake for breakfast, and Richie brings home Arnold's soft-serve frozen custard to be eaten out of the tub or transformed into sundaes and malts. Look twice before you step through the back door and into the kitchen—you never know who's on the other side indulging in another kind of treat, "Sugar Lips"!

Mrs. Piccalo's Candy Apple Fluff

Officer Kirk tries to shut down the dance at Arnold's. Again. He's not a bad guy but a little obsessed with the idea that Fonzie is a criminal. The gang enlists the entire neighborhood—including the Piccalos—to try a bit of "dessert diplomacy" before they tell him to "Sit on it!"

PREP TIME: *20 minutes* | **CHILL TIME:** *60 minutes* | **YIELD:** *6 to 8 servings* | **DIETARY NOTE:** *Vegetarian, Gluten-Free*

1 box (3.4 ounces) instant vanilla pudding mix

2 cups cold milk

4 medium-sized apples, peeled, cored, and chopped into small pieces

4 chocolate-coated peanut, nougat, and caramel candy bars, chopped into small pieces

1 cup whipped cream or whipped topping

½ cup shelled, salted peanuts (optional)

Caramel sauce or chocolate sauce for drizzling (for optional garnish)

In a large mixing bowl, prepare the vanilla pudding according to the instructions on the package, using the cold milk. Whisk vigorously for about 2 minutes until the pudding thickens.

Fold the chopped apples and candy bar pieces into the prepared vanilla pudding until they are evenly distributed.

Gently fold in the whipped cream or whipped topping, being careful not to overmix so that the fluff remains light and airy.

Transfer the apple, vanilla pudding, candy bar, and whipped cream mixture to a serving dish or individual dessert cups.

Sprinkle peanuts and drizzle caramel sauce or chocolate sauce over the top, if desired.

Chill the dessert in the refrigerator for at least 1 hour, or until ready to serve.

NOTE

Nut allergy? Use a candy bar without nuts.

Trivia

When Fonzie has to fake his death to uncover the real bad guys, Officer Kirk pays his respects to "Widow Fonzarelli," who is really Fonzie in disguise. It's not the first time Fonzie has had to dress in women's clothing! How many times has Fonz donned a disguise?

Anytime Pumpkin Pie

When is the pie-in-the-face joke not funny? When the pie is aimed at Fonz's face! Choose wisely and eat this rich and spicy pie instead of throwing it. Well, maybe aim at Potsie. He is now the Leopard Lodge pledge master and made Fonzie wear a fuzzy bunny suit to Arnold's.

PREP TIME: *30 to 45 minutes* | **CHILL TIME:** *30 minutes plus 2 hours* | **COOK TIME:** *45 to 50 minutes*
YIELD: *8 servings* | **DIETARY NOTE:** *Vegetarian*

INGREDIENTS FOR THE CRUST:

1¼ cups all-purpose flour

½ teaspoon salt

½ cup (1 stick) unsalted butter, cold and cut into small cubes

2 to 3 tablespoons ice water

INGREDIENTS FOR THE FILLING:

2 cups pumpkin puree (canned or homemade)

1 cup heavy cream

½ cup packed brown sugar

¼ cup granulated sugar

3 large eggs

1 teaspoon vanilla extract

1 teaspoon ground cinnamon

½ teaspoon ground ginger

¼ teaspoon ground nutmeg

¼ teaspoon ground cloves

½ teaspoon salt

Trivia

It's now the mid-'60s and Potsie is working with Mr. Cunningham at the hardware store. Mr. C. also recruited Potsie to join the Lodge. What's Potsie's secret Lodge name?

TO MAKE THE CRUST:

In a mixing bowl, whisk together the flour and salt.

Add the cold butter cubes and using a pastry cutter, cut the butter into the flour mixture until it resembles coarse crumbs.

Gradually add ice water, 1 tablespoon at a time, and mix until the dough comes together.

Gather the dough into a ball, flatten it into a disk, wrap it in plastic wrap, and refrigerate for at least 30 minutes. While dough is chilling, preheat oven to 375°F and make the filling.

TO MAKE FILLING:

In a large mixing bowl, whisk together the pumpkin puree, heavy cream, brown sugar, granulated sugar, eggs, vanilla extract, cinnamon, ginger, nutmeg, cloves, and salt until well combined and smooth.

TO ASSEMBLE:

On a lightly floured surface, roll out the chilled dough into a circle slightly larger than your pie dish.

Carefully transfer the rolled-out dough to a 9-inch pie dish, gently pressing it into the bottom and sides. Trim any excess dough and crimp the edges decoratively.

Pour the pumpkin custard filling into the prebaked or unbaked pie crust, spreading it evenly.

Place the pie on a baking sheet and transfer it to the oven.

Bake for about 45 to 50 minutes, or until the filling is set and the center of the pie no longer jiggles when gently shaken. (If the edges of the crust start to brown too quickly, cover them with foil or a pie crust shield.)

Remove the pie from the oven and let it cool completely on a wire rack.

Once cooled, refrigerate the pie for at least 2 hours, or overnight, to allow the flavors to meld and the custard to set.

Serve a dollop of whipped cream on each slice of pie, if desired.

Chocolate Layer Cake

Birthday cakes, wedding cakes, cakes in the shape of Arnold's . . . on *Happy Days*, special occasions require cake. Is Tuesday a special occasion? It can be with this everyday chocolate cake Mrs. C. whips up in an hour. Everyone will line up to get a slice of this baked deliciousness . . . even if a burlesque dancer isn't serving it.

PREP TIME: *30 minutes* | **CHILL TIME:** *60 minutes* | **COOK TIME:** *30 to 35 minutes* | **YIELD:** *8 to 12 servings* | **DIETARY NOTE:** *Vegetarian*

INGREDIENTS FOR THE CAKE:

2 cups all-purpose flour

1¾ cups granulated sugar

¾ cup unsweetened cocoa powder

1½ teaspoons baking powder

1½ teaspoons baking soda

1 teaspoon salt

2 large eggs

1 cup milk

½ cup neutral vegetable oil

2 teaspoons vanilla extract

1 cup boiling water

INGREDIENTS FOR THE FROSTING:

1½ cups unsalted butter, softened

3½ cups powdered sugar

1 cup unsweetened cocoa powder

½ cup heavy cream

1 teaspoon vanilla extract

Chocolate shavings or sprinkles (optional)

NOTE

For an extra-chocolate-y cake and frosting, use dark or "black" cocoa powder. You can prepare the cakes a day ahead or even freeze for up to 3 months, then prepare frosting and assemble when you want to serve.

Preheat oven to 350°F. Grease and flour two 9-inch round cake pans.

In a large mixing bowl, whisk together the flour, granulated sugar, cocoa powder, baking powder, baking soda, and salt until well combined.

Add the eggs, milk, vegetable oil, and vanilla extract to the dry ingredients. Mix on medium speed with an electric mixer until the batter is smooth and well combined, about 2 minutes.

Reduce the mixer speed to low and carefully pour in the boiling water. Mix until the batter is evenly combined. The batter will be thin.

Divide the batter equally between the prepared cake pans.

Place pans in the oven and bake for 30 to 35 minutes, or until a toothpick inserted into the center of the cakes comes out clean.

Remove the cakes from the oven and let them cool in the pans for 10 minutes. Then transfer them to a wire rack to cool completely.

While the cakes are cooling, prepare the frosting: In a large mixing bowl, beat the softened butter until creamy.

Gradually add the powdered sugar and cocoa powder, mixing on low speed until well combined. Then, increase the speed to medium and beat for an additional 2 to 3 minutes.

Add the heavy cream and vanilla extract and beat on medium-high speed until the frosting is light and fluffy, about 3 to 4 minutes.

Once the cakes are completely cooled, place one layer on a serving plate or cake stand. Spread a generous amount of frosting evenly over the top.

Place the second layer on top of the frosted layer. Use the remaining frosting to cover the top and sides of the cake. Use an offset spatula or the back of a spoon to create a smooth, even surface.

If desired, decorate cake with chocolate shavings or sprinkles.

Chill the cake in the refrigerator for at least 1 hour before serving to allow the frosting to set.

This cake can be stored at room temperature in an airtight container for up to 3 days or refrigerated for up to 1 week. Bring it to room temperature before serving for the best taste and texture.

Junior Chipmunk's Poke Cake

A quick and delicious cake easy enough for Joanie's Junior Chipmunk troop to make. Will you earn a badge for making this cake? Probably not, but Fonzie would call you a vision of loveliness when you bring one over for his birthday.

PREP TIME: *20 minutes* | **CHILL TIME:** *3 hours* | **COOK TIME:** *25 to 35 minutes*
YIELD: *12 to 16 servings* | **DIETARY NOTE:** *Vegetarian*

INGREDIENTS FOR CAKE:
1 box (18.25 ounces) yellow or white cake mix (Do not include the rest of the back-of-box ingredients.)

3 eggs

½ cup melted butter

1 cup whole milk

INGREDIENTS FOR PUDDING TOPPING:
1 box (3.4 ounces) instant pudding mix (flavor of your choice)

2 cups cold milk

Whipped cream (optional)

Chocolate shavings or sprinkles (optional)

Preheat oven to 325°F. Grease and flour a 9-by-13-inch glass baking dish.

In a large bowl, add the cake mix, eggs, butter, and milk. Mix on low speed with hand-held or stand mixer until batter is thoroughly blended.

Pour the prepared cake batter into the greased and floured baking pan. Smooth the top with a spatula.

Place cake in the oven and bake for 25 minutes then check for doneness. (Return to the oven and bake until a toothpick inserted into the center comes out clean.) Remove from oven and cool in pan for 10 minutes.

While the cake is baking, prepare the pudding. In a mixing bowl, combine the instant pudding mix and cold milk. Whisk vigorously for about 2 minutes until the pudding thickens.

When the cake has cooled but is still warm, use the handle of a wooden spoon to poke holes all over the top of the cake. Make sure the holes go all the way through to the bottom.

Slowly pour the prepared pudding over the cake, making sure the pudding fills the holes and spreads evenly across the surface.

Place cake in refrigerator for 1 hour to cool and set pudding. Once the cake has cooled, top with whipped cream spread evenly over the pudding layer. Add chocolate shavings or sprinkles, if desired. Return to refrigerator and chill for at least 2 hours to meld flavors.

NOTE
Substitute your favorite instant flavored gelatin for a colorful and fruity cake.

Trivia
Fonzie has one hero. Who is it?

Blueberry Shortcake

Whoa, Shortcake! Slow down there! Mr. Cunningham thinks Joanie is growing up too fast, but when you're the youngest of the family, there's a lot of catching up to do . . . boys, dates, school, dates. Joanie's sass (she takes after Mrs. Cunningham's side of the family) keeps everyone on their toes. Peace reigns at the dinner table when this old-fashioned shortcake appears.

PREP TIME: *30 minutes* | **CHILL TIME:** *15 minutes* | **COOK TIME:** *15 to 20 minutes* | **YIELD:** *12 servings* | **DIETARY NOTE:** *Vegetarian*

INGREDIENTS FOR SHORTCAKE:

4 cups all-purpose flour

3 tablespoons baking powder

1 teaspoon salt

2 tablespoons butter

16 ounces heavy cream

INGREDIENTS FOR TOPPING:

6 cups fresh or frozen blueberries

1 cup 100% pure maple syrup

Arnold's World-Famous Frozen Soft-Serve Custard (page 165), vanilla ice cream, or whipped cream (optional)

Trivia

Marion would never have served Strawberry Shortcake to her family. Why?

TO MAKE SHORTCAKES:

Preheat oven to 400°F.

In a large bowl, sift together the flour, baking powder, and salt until thoroughly blended.

Using a pastry cutter (or food processor), rub the butter into the flour mixture until it becomes pebbly.

Add the heavy cream and mix with a large spoon or hands. Work the dough until it is combined, being careful not to overwork it. The dough will be soft and somewhat sticky.

Take about ¼ cup of dough and shape it into a rough ball using your hands. Place the dough balls on jelly roll pans lined with parchment paper, spacing them approximately 2 inches apart. Pat down each ball until it reaches a height of about an inch.

Cover the pan with a cotton cloth and set it on top of the hot stove to rise for about 15 minutes.

Remove the cloth and place the pans into the oven. Bake for about 20 minutes. Check the biscuits at the 15-minute mark and adjust baking time accordingly.

TO MAKE TOPPING:

While shortcakes are baking, place rinsed or defrosted blueberries into medium saucepan over medium heat. Gently stir as blueberries cook for about 5 minutes or until they begin to release juice.

Add the maple syrup and cook for another 10 minutes while stirring. Remove from heat when blueberries have released their juice.

Mash or puree mixture to preferred consistency. Set aside.

TO ASSEMBLE:

Remove the biscuits from the oven and serve immediately by splitting the biscuit shortcake in half and ladling with about ½ cup of blueberry mixture per shortcake.

Cover with the other half of the shortcake. Top the entire Blueberry Shortcake with a scoop of frozen custard, vanilla ice cream, or whipped cream.

Patton Vocational High School Cafeteria Slab Cheesecake

It's a rough start for Principal Roger Phillips with Roach and the other boys at George S. Patton Vocational High School vandalizing his car. Maybe if Roger added this sure-fire dessert to the school lunch menu, the boys wouldn't cause so much trouble. Is Roger still a nerd? Yes, but he's learning.

PREP TIME: *30 minutes* | **CHILL TIME:** *4 hours* | **COOK TIME:** *50 to 60 minutes* | **YIELD:** *24 to 32 servings* | **DIETARY NOTE:** *Vegetarian*

4 cups graham cracker crumbs

1 cup (2 sticks) unsalted butter, melted

½ cup granulated sugar

32 ounces cream cheese, softened

1½ cups granulated sugar

4 large eggs

1 cup sour cream

¼ cup all-purpose flour

1 tablespoon vanilla extract

1 cup sour cream

2 tablespoons granulated sugar

1 teaspoon vanilla extract

Preheat oven to 325°F. Line 13-by-18-inch jelly roll pan with parchment paper.

In a medium bowl, combine the graham cracker crumbs, melted butter, and sugar for the crust. Mix until all the crumbs are coated with butter.

Press the crumb mixture firmly into the bottom of the prepared pan to form an even layer. Set aside.

In a large mixing bowl, beat the cream cheese and granulated sugar together until smooth and creamy.

Add the eggs, one at a time, beating well after each addition. Scrape down the sides of the bowl as needed. Mix in the sour cream, flour, and vanilla extract until all the ingredients are fully incorporated and the batter is smooth.

Pour the cheesecake filling over the prepared crust in the baking pan. Use a spatula to spread the filling evenly. (Batter will come up to edge or just below the edge of pan.)

Place in the oven and bake for about 45 to 50 minutes, or until the edges are set and the center is slightly jiggly. While the cheesecake is baking, prepare the topping.

In a small bowl, whisk together the sour cream, granulated sugar, and vanilla extract until well combined.

After the initial baking time, remove the cheesecake from the oven and carefully spread the sour cream topping over the hot cheesecake.

Return the cheesecake to the oven and bake for an additional 5 minutes. Remove the cheesecake from the oven and let it cool completely in the baking pan on a wire rack.

Once cooled, cover the pan with plastic wrap and refrigerate the cheesecake for at least 4 hours, or overnight, to allow it to fully set and chill.

Before serving, carefully lift the cheesecake out of the pan using the edges of the parchment paper. Cut into desired portions.

Trivia

What actor, who has a reputation for unpredictable improvisation and went on to big film roles in the '80s and '90s, played Roach?

Ralph Malph's Cherries Jubilee

Potsie and Ralph are the best of friends but the worst of roommates as we find out in season five. Potsie can't even make a TV dinner so Ralph appoints himself head chef, but is it food if you can't eat it? Make this Cherries Jubilee for your best friend, just don't set the kitchen ablaze!

PREP TIME: *10 to 20 minutes* | **COOK TIME:** *5 to 8 minutes* | **YIELD:** *4 to 6 servings* | **DIETARY NOTE:** *Vegetarian, Gluten-Free*

- 2 cups fresh or frozen pitted cherries
- ¼ cup granulated sugar
- 2 tablespoons unsalted butter
- 2 tablespoons brandy or cherry liqueur
- 1 teaspoon lemon juice
- ½ teaspoon vanilla extract
- Vanilla ice cream or pound cake, for serving

═ NOTE ═

The alcohol in Cherries Jubilee is optional, but adds a rich flavor to the dish. If you prefer to omit it, substitute with cherry or orange juice. Adjust the sweetness by adding more or less sugar, depending on your taste preferences.

In a medium-sized saucepan, combine the cherries and granulated sugar. Cook over medium heat, stirring occasionally, until the sugar dissolves and the cherries release their juices.

Add the butter to the saucepan and continue to cook the cherries for another 2 to 3 minutes until the butter melts and the mixture thickens slightly.

Remove the saucepan from the heat and carefully add the brandy or cherry liqueur. Be cautious as the alcohol may cause the mixture to flame. If desired, you can use a long match or lighter to ignite the alcohol for a dramatic flambé effect. Allow the flames to burn out naturally or carefully extinguish them by covering the pan with a lid.

Return the saucepan to low heat and simmer the cherries for an additional 2 to 3 minutes, stirring gently. (This will help thicken the sauce and cook off any remaining alcohol.)

Stir in the lemon juice and vanilla extract. Remove the saucepan from the heat.

Serve the Cherries Jubilee warm over a scoop of vanilla ice cream or alongside slices of pound cake.

Ha-Cha-Cha Brownies

The surprise hint of spicy heat makes these brownies perfect for Ralph. Too much spice may result in zero laughs but take Ralph's advice: Everything is funny when you're wearing a rubber nose. He's still got it!

PREP TIME: *15 to 20 minutes* | **COOK TIME:** *30 to 35 minutes* | **YIELD:** *12 to 16 servings* | **DIETARY NOTE:** *Vegetarian*

1 cup unsalted butter, melted

2 cups granulated sugar

4 large eggs

1 teaspoon vanilla extract

1 cup all-purpose flour

½ cup unsweetened cocoa powder

½ cup chocolate wheat farina cereal

½ teaspoon ground cinnamon (optional)

½ teaspoon chile powder (optional)

½ teaspoon salt

1 tablespoon sifted powder sugar (optional)

Preheat oven to 350°F. Grease and flour a 9-by-9-inch baking pan.

In a large mixing bowl, combine the melted butter and granulated sugar. Mix until well combined.

Add the eggs one at a time, mixing well after each addition. Stir in the vanilla extract.

In a separate bowl, whisk together the flour, cocoa powder, chocolate farina cereal, cinnamon, chile powder, and salt.

Gradually add the dry ingredient mixture to the wet ingredients, stirring until just combined. Do not overmix.

Pour the brownie batter into the prepared baking pan and spread it evenly.

Place pan in the oven and bake for about 30 to 35 minutes, or until a toothpick inserted into the center comes out with a few moist crumbs. Be careful not to overbake.

When done, remove the brownies from the oven and let them cool in the pan on a wire rack.

When completely cooled, sprinkle with 1 tablespoon of powdered sugar and cut into squares or rectangles.

NOTE

Omit the cinnamon and chile powder for less spicy brownies. Increase chile powder by ½ teaspoon for more Ha-Cha-Cha!

Trivia

Ralph gets his sense of humor from his father, Mickey Malph. What's Dr. Malph's profession?

"Bag" Zombroski's Demon Zucchini Bread

Bag was a decent drummer and a better prankster. Was he Richie's friend or enemy? Hard to tell. But he once challenged the guys to "get a kiss by midnight," and the loser had to run through Arnold's parking lot in their underwear.

PREP TIME: *30 minutes* | **COOK TIME:** *55 to 65 minutes* | **YIELD:** *1 loaf, about 8 to 10 servings* | **DIETARY NOTE:** *Vegetarian*

2 cups all-purpose flour

1 teaspoon baking soda

1 teaspoon baking powder

½ teaspoon kosher salt

1 teaspoon ground cinnamon

½ teaspoon ground nutmeg

½ cup granulated sugar

½ cup packed light brown sugar

½ cup vegetable oil

2 large eggs

1 teaspoon vanilla extract

2 cups grated zucchini (about 2 medium-sized zucchinis)

½ cup dried cranberries

½ cup chopped walnuts or pecans (optional)

Preheat oven to 350°F. Grease and flour a 9-by-5-inch loaf pan.

In a medium-sized bowl, whisk together the flour, baking soda, baking powder, salt, cinnamon, and nutmeg. Set aside.

In a large mixing bowl, beat the granulated sugar, brown sugar, and vegetable oil together until well combined.

Add the eggs one at a time, beating well after each addition. Stir in the vanilla extract.

Gradually add the dry ingredient mixture to the wet ingredients, mixing just until combined. Avoid overmixing.

Fold in the grated zucchini, cranberries, and walnuts (if using) until evenly distributed throughout the batter.

Pour the batter into the prepared loaf pan, spreading it evenly.

Place pan in the oven and bake for 55 to 65 minutes, or until a toothpick inserted into the center of the bread comes out clean or with just a few moist crumbs.

Remove the bread from the oven and let it cool in the pan for 10 minutes. Then, transfer it to a wire rack to cool completely.

Once completely cooled, slice and serve with a spread of butter.

═ NOTE ═

Store any leftover zucchini bread in an airtight container at room temperature for up to 3 days, or in the refrigerator for up to a week.

Trivia

The bet was between Bag, Richie, Potsie, and Ralph. Who won?

Grandpa Cunningham's Irish Fruitcake

Grandpa Sean "Cap" Cunningham shared this recipe with his favorite daughter-in-law, Marion. It's a rich, fruity, nutty, and delicious taste of Ireland that can even be eaten for breakfast. Marion always makes it for Cap because the long cooking time means a longer visit with "Sonny," um, sorry, Howard.

PREP TIME: *45 minutes* | **CHILL TIME:** *1 hour* | **COOK TIME:** *3 hours* | **YIELD:** *2 loaf-sized cakes* | **DIETARY NOTE:** *Vegetarian*

2 cups all-purpose flour

1 teaspoon baking soda

Pinch of nutmeg

1 pound high-fat butter, 82% to 84% butterfat

2 cups white sugar

4 eggs

3 tablespoons lemon juice

12 ounces Irish stout beer (non-alcohol Irish stout beer can be substituted)

2 cups frozen cherries, defrosted and drained

1 cup frozen strawberries, defrosted and drained

1 tablespoon lemon zest

2 tablespoons orange zest

1 cup dried cranberries

1 cup sultanas (golden raisins)

1 cup dried apricots, chopped

½ cup dried or fresh currants

½ cup sliced almonds

½ cup chopped walnuts

¼ cup (½ stick) regular butter (for pan preparation)

In a large bowl, sift flour, baking soda, and nutmeg together. Cut in butter with pastry cutter until mixture is a pebbly consistency. Cut in the sugar.

In a separate smaller bowl, crack the eggs and beat them together. Mix in lemon juice. Add this mixture to the dry mixture and stir just until batter comes together.

Add Irish stout beer and stir until well combined.

Add cherries and mix until evenly distributed. Then add the strawberries, orange zest, and lemon zest, and mix well.

Add the dried fruits and nuts to the batter and stir until evenly incorporated. (The mixture consistency should be like pancake batter.)

Cover bowl with plastic wrap and rest on counter for 1 hour.

Preheat oven to 275°F.

Generously butter bread loaf pans. Using a large ladle, scoop the batter into the baking pans until ¾ full.

Place the pans on cookie sheet and place into the oven. Bake for 3 hours, or until a toothpick inserted into the center of the cake comes out clean. Keep baking until the toothpick comes out clean, checking every 15 minutes.

Remove from the oven and let the cakes cool completely in pans.

Serve in a bowl with freshly made hand-whipped cream and a cup of coffee.

NOTE

Grandpa Cunningham's Irish Fruitcake is a hybrid of an English-style pudding and traditional fruitcake.

Trivia

Captain Sean Cunningham is played by an entertainment legend with ties to Ron Howard. Who played Cap Cunningham?

Mork's Red, White, and Blue Gelatin

Would you like to live on Ork? No? *Shazbot*! Say *nanu* to Mork from Ork who travels through space and time to learn about average American life. Richie's life will be anything but humdrum, but will anyone believe him? Only The Fonz, who tries to teach Mork about, you know, *the ladies*. If Mork had talked to Mrs. C. instead of freezing her, she would have sent him home to Ork with this all-American dessert.

PREP TIME: *30 minutes* | **CHILL TIME:** *about 60 minutes plus additional 4 hours* | **COOK TIME:** *15 to 20 minutes* | **YIELD:** *4 servings*

1 box (3 ounces) instant blue gelatin (such as blue raspberry)

2 envelopes (about 4 teaspoons) unflavored gelatin

½ cup cold water

1 cup boiling water

½ cup granulated sugar

1 box (3 ounces) instant red gelatin (such as strawberry or cherry)

1 cup heavy cream

1 teaspoon vanilla extract

Fresh strawberries and blueberries, for garnish (optional)

NOTE

Change the flavors and colors of gelatin to celebrate any party theme.

Trivia

Fonz arranges for Mork to go on a date so Mork can learn about love. Who is Mork's blind date?

In a medium bowl, prepare the blue gelatin according to the package instructions. Pour mixture into a 9-by-13-inch glass baking dish or into 4 equal parts per individual serving dishes to create the layers.

Place in freezer for 20 minutes to quick set. While the blue layer is chilling, prepare the white layer.

In a small bowl, sprinkle the unflavored gelatin over the cold water and let it sit for 1 to 2 minutes to bloom.

In a separate bowl, combine the boiling water and granulated sugar, stirring until the sugar is dissolved.

Add the bloomed gelatin mixture to the hot water and sugar mixture, stirring until the gelatin is completely dissolved. Stir in the heavy cream and vanilla extract until well combined. Allow the white gelatin mixture to cool to room temperature.

Remove blue layer from freezer. Gently pour the white gelatin mixture over the set blue gelatin. Be careful not to pour it too quickly or it may disrupt the blue layer. Place in freezer for 20 minutes to quick set.

While the white layer is chilling, prepare red gelatin according to the package instructions.

Remove set blue and white layers from freezer. Gently pour the red gelatin mixture over the set white gelatin. Be careful not to pour it too quickly or it may disrupt the white layer.

Refrigerate until fully set, about 4 hours.

Once the final layer is set, garnish with fresh strawberries and blueberries, arranging them in a patriotic pattern if desired.

FROM **Arnold's** MENU

All days are happy days—especially when paired with Arnold's desserts!

ARNOLD'S WORLD-FAMOUS FROZEN SOFT-SERVE CUSTARD

Arnold's soft serve is not like any other because it's not ice cream . . . it's frozen custard. Delicious and decadent, eat it in a dish or use as the base for all of Arnold's frozen treats. Not recommended—drinking twelve malts in a row. Potsie is such a Potsie!

PREP TIME: *10 minutes* | **COOK TIME:** *15 to 20 minutes* | **CHILL TIME:** *4 to 6 hours* | **YIELD:** *4 servings* | **DIETARY NOTE:** *Vegetarian, Gluten-Free*

2 cups whole milk

1 cup heavy cream

¾ cup granulated sugar

4 large egg yolks

1 teaspoon pure vanilla extract

═══ NOTE ═══

Create flavored frozen custard by adding ingredients like chocolate chips, crushed cookies, or fruit puree before freezing the custard. Just fold in your desired mix-ins gently before transferring the custard to the freezer.

Trivia

Anson Williams, who played Potsie for all eleven seasons, rarely acts today but still works in television. What does he do?

In a medium saucepan over medium-low heat, combine the milk and heavy cream. Stir occasionally to prevent scorching. Heat the mixture until warm. Remove from heat.

While the milk and cream mixture is heating, in a separate large bowl, whisk together the granulated sugar and egg yolks until well combined and slightly thickened.

When the milk mixture is warmed, slowly add ½ cup of the milk mixture into the egg mixture while continuously whisking to temper the egg yolks.

Pour the tempered egg and milk mixture back into the saucepan with the remaining milk mixture and cook over low heat. Stir constantly with a wooden spoon or heatproof spatula, scraping the bottom of the pan for about 8 to 10 minutes, until the mixture coats the back of a spoon.

Remove from the heat and stir in the vanilla extract. Let the mixture cool to room temperature.

Once the custard base has cooled, transfer it to an airtight freezer-safe container or a loaf pan. Cover the container tightly with plastic wrap, making sure the plastic wrap touches the surface of the custard to prevent "skin" from forming.

Place the container in the freezer for about 2 to 3 hours, or until the edges of the custard begin to freeze.

Remove the container from the freezer and use a fork or a whisk to vigorously mix and break up any ice crystals that have formed. This helps create a smoother texture.

Return the container to the freezer and repeat the process of mixing every 30 minutes for the next 2 to 3 hours, or until the custard is completely frozen and has a creamy, soft-serve consistency.

Once the frozen custard reaches the desired consistency, it is ready to serve. You can scoop it into cones or use to make one of the following Arnold's treats.

THICK MILWAUKEE MALT

A Thick Milwaukee Malt is the secret to Fonzie's Kazotsky Kick. It's the boost you need after pushing a motorcycle twelve miles before the dance marathon.

PREP TIME: *15 minutes* | **YIELD:** *2 servings* | **DIETARY NOTE:** *Vegetarian*

2 cups Arnold's World-Famous Frozen Soft-Serve Custard (page 165)

¾ cup whole milk

¼ cup malted milk powder

2 tablespoons chocolate syrup

Whipped cream, for topping (optional)

Maraschino cherries, for garnish (optional)

In a blender, combine the frozen custard, whole milk, malted milk powder, and chocolate syrup.

Blend on high speed until smooth and creamy.

Taste the milkshake and adjust the sweetness or thickness by adding more malted milk powder or milk if desired. Once you achieve the desired consistency and taste, pour the malted milkshake into 2 tall glasses.

Top each milkshake with a dollop of whipped cream and garnish with a maraschino cherry. Serve the malted milkshakes immediately with a straw.

=== NOTE ===

You can customize the Milwaukee Malt by adding additional mix-ins such as crushed cookies, chocolate chips, or flavored syrups.

BANANA BOAT

Here's a tip from Fonzie: Get the Banana Boat and share it with your favorite date. You'll be heading up to Inspiration Point in no time.

PREP TIME: *15 minutes* | **YIELD:** *2 servings* | **DIETARY NOTE:** *Vegetarian, Gluten-Free*

2 ripe bananas

2 cups Arnold's World-Famous Frozen Soft-Serve Custard (page 165)

¼ cup chocolate sauce

¼ cup caramel sauce

Whipped cream, for topping

Spanish peanuts, for garnish (optional)

Maraschino cherry, for garnish (optional)

Peel the bananas and slice them lengthwise into halves. Place each banana half in a separate serving dish or boat-shaped bowl.

Scoop a generous amount of frozen custard onto each banana boat, covering the bananas completely.

Drizzle the chocolate sauce and caramel sauce over the frozen custard.

Top each banana boat sundae with a dollop of whipped cream.

Sprinkle Spanish peanuts over the whipped cream and finish with a maraschino cherry.

CRA-A-ZY CRUNCH SUNDAE

Hard to believe Arnold's Sundae is only 35 cents!
It's worth at least twice that much.

PREP TIME: *20 minutes* | **COOK TIME:** *8 minutes for strawberry crunch* | **YIELD:** *2 servings* | **DIETARY NOTE:** *Vegetarian*

INGREDIENTS FOR CRA-A-ZY CRUNCH SUNDAE:

½ cup Arnold's Toffee Crunch (see recipe)

2 cups Arnold's World-Famous Frozen Soft-Serve Custard (page 165)

½ cup Strawberry Crunch (see recipe)

Whipped cream, for topping

Maraschino cherries, for garnish

INGREDIENTS FOR ARNOLD'S TOFFEE CRUNCH:

1½ cups (12 ounces) butter toffee covered peanuts

½ cup (4 ounces) multi-colored sprinkles

INGREDIENTS FOR STRAWBERRY CRUNCH:

24 (1 package) vanilla sandwich cookies

1 box (3 ounces) strawberry gelatin

4 tablespoons melted butter

TO MAKE ARNOLD'S TOFFEE CRUNCH:

In a food processor, pulse the toffee peanuts until coarsely chopped.

Pour the chopped peanuts into a shallow dish and add the sprinkles. Mix.

Store in an air-tight container for 1 week.

TO MAKE STRAWBERRY CRUNCH:

Preheat oven to 350°F.

In a food processor, place the cookies and pulse until reduced to small crumbles. (Alternately: Place cookies in a plastic storage bag and beat with rolling pin.)

In a medium bowl, combine the crumbled cookies, strawberry gelatin powder, and melted butter. Mix gently until well combined.

Line baking sheet with parchment paper. Spread the mixture onto the baking sheet, evenly distributed.

Place sheet in the oven and bake for 8 minutes.

Remove from the oven and cool before using.

TO ASSEMBLE THE SUNDAE:

In a serving dish or bowl, add a ½-cup layer of Arnold's Toffee Crunch at the bottom.

Add 2 scoops (about 1 cup) of Arnold's Frozen Custard on top of Toffee Crunch.

Sprinkle a layer of Strawberry Crunch over the frozen custard.

Top the sundae with a dollop of whipped cream and a maraschino cherry.

Holiday and Celebration Menus

FOURTH OF JULY COOKOUT

Dude Ranch Baked Barbeque Beans

Cunningham Coleslaw

Leopard Lodge Oven-Roasted Corn on the Cob

Leopard Lodge Potato Salad (Howard's
German Style or Marion's American Style)

Slow-Roasted Brisket

Mork's Red, White, and Blue Gelatin

JOANIE'S TEENAGE DREAM BIRTHDAY PARTY

Momo Burgers

Grilled Cheese with Peanuts

Arnold's Cherry Limeade

Ha-Cha-Cha Brownies topped with Arnold's
World-Famous Frozen Soft-Serve Custard

THANKSGIVING

Wine-Soaked Roast Turkey and Gravy

Kelp Family Chestnut Stuffing

Cranberry Sauce

Mr. C.'s "Feed the Platoon" Candied Yams

Green Beans Almondine

Anytime Pumpkin Pie

Holiday Cider Punch

CHRISTMAS

Sunday Baked Ham

Fresh-Buttered Sweet Peas

Mushroom Wild Rice

"Swedish" Meatballs

Grandpa Cunningham's Irish Fruitcake

Food Fight Rolls and Herb Butter

"Spiked" Orange Eggnog

Afterword

Happy Days had a profound cultural impact beyond the original broadcast of 255 episodes between 1974 to 1984. Through the power of syndication and now on-demand streaming, old and new fans alike spend time with Fonzie and the Cunninghams. The show re-popularized drive-in restaurants, jukeboxes, poodle skirts, and sock hops. The show came to define the American Dream during eras of social and political turbulence while offering comfort and timeless laughs. *Happy Days* represents the best of America: the can-do spirit, the resilience, and the joy we share celebrating our families.

Food was a center of the *Happy Days* world that reflected and inspired our ideas of who—and what—America is. The Cunninghams' kitchen was a culinary sanctuary, presided over by Marion Cunningham, the epitome of the loving TV mom. Her homemade dishes were an edible manifestation of her warmth and affection. Whether it was her legendary meatloaf or her fluffy pancakes, the Cunninghams' kitchen proved that love truly does have a secret ingredient, and it's often butter.

Arnold's re-introduced diner-style delights and the power of shared communal spaces to grow friendships and community. The iconic drive-in has inspired hundreds of restaurants throughout the United States and once starred in an equally iconic music video by the band Weezer! *Happy Days* showed us that food has the power to bring people together, make us laugh, and create lasting memories. So, let's raise a Thick Milwaukee Malt (page 166) to the food of *Happy Days* as we give the last word to Howard Cunningham . . .

"Thank you all for being part of our family . . . To happy days."

Trivia Answers

PAGE 9: "DUDE RANCH" BREAKFAST SKILLET
She's an accomplished trick-rider! She and her dancing horse wowed the rodeo crowds with their display.

PAGE 11: BLUEBERRY HILL PANCAKES
Fats Domino added his trademark New Orleans–style rockin' piano style to the 1940 Glenn Miller Orchestra hit and brought it back to the charts for a new generation of listeners.

PAGE 14: CUNNINGHAM'S STRENGTHENING SCOTTISH OATMEAL
It was Arnold! Matsuo Takahashi is Arnold's real name. When he bought the restaurant, the sign was already in place, so he changed his name rather than spend money to buy a new sign.

PAGE 21: PORK SAUSAGE APPLE ROULADE ROAST
Cathy Silvers played Jenny. And the sole appearance of Mr. Piccalo was played by Cathy's real-life father, actor and comedian Phil Silvers.

PAGE 23: LEOPARD LODGE POTATO SALAD
Mr. Wilson was played by Ron Howard's father, Rance Howard.

PAGE 26: CUNNINGHAM COLESLAW
Anson Williams, who played Potsie Weber.

PAGE 27: WEDGE SALAD
Charles is his first name.

PAGE 29: PFISTER SALAD
Linda Purl played Richie's girlfriend Gloria in four episodes during season two.

PAGE 31: HOMEMADE HONEY-CINNAMON PEANUT BUTTER AND RASPBERRY JAM SANDWICH
In 1917 during World War I when citizens were asked to help the cause and stop eating meat on Mondays, peanut butter became a popular substitute for meat protein.

PAGE 35: RICHIE'S FAVORITE SARDINE SANDWICH
Richie was stationed in Greenland.

PAGE 36: HAWAIIAN LŪ`AU CLUB SANDWICH WITH SECRET SANDWICH SPREAD
It's not because of drumsticks! It's because he's skinny as a stick.

PAGE 38: "FROM THE STORE" SANDWICH BREAD
Richie's dad, Mr. Cunningham, was also attending the show!

PAGE 41: THE BOPPER AND BIG BOPPER BURGERS
The burgers are named after J.P. Richardson, aka The Big Bopper, who rose to fame with his hit, "Chantilly Lace," in 1958. Richardson tragically died in the same plane crash that killed Richie Valens and Buddy Holly on February 3, 1959.

PAGE 45: ARNOLD'S SLOW COOKER CHILI
He went to Italy on his first vacation ever. Problem: He didn't know the Italian word for "razor."

PAGE 46: MOMO BURGERS
The past two times he was best man, the wedding was canceled. Once due to a fist fight and once on account of "wandering lips" that wandered onto Fonz when the groom's back was turned!

PAGE 48: THE BIG "A" SLOPPY JOE SANDWICH
Al's former flame was Rosa Coletti.

PAGE 49: DELUX B.L.T.
The cooks were Fredrick, Fonzie's cousin Angie for one episode, Clarence, and Chachi. Fred never appeared on camera while Clarence appeared once in season ten. Chachi began working as a part-time waiter and cook during season seven.

PAGE 51: SPLISH-SPLASH TUNA MELT SANDWICH
The band remained unnamed for the entire duration of the show, but the guys often introduced Potsie as the "Velvet Cloud." The nickname is a reference to popular crooner of the era Mel Tormé, who was known as the "Velvet Fog."

PAGE 52: GRILLED CHEESE WITH PEANUTS
They dressed up in a two-person cow costume with Fonzie at the front and Richie bringing up the rear.

PAGE 56: MALACHI CRUNCH SPICY SNACK MIX
Pinky drives a 1955 Cadillac and gets clobbered by the Malachi Brothers.

PAGE 59: JUMP THE SHARK CANDY SUSHI
Fonzie meets a talent scout on the hunt for the next James Dean and wants him to come to Hollywood for a screen test. Fonz invites the Cunninghams to join him on his California adventure.

PAGE 60: FIG BAR COOKIES
Fonzie reminds Potsie that he easily remembered the lyrics to hundreds of songs, and if he set the names of all the human bones to a melody, he could sing his way to an "A." Psst: Potsie passed the exam.

PAGE 65: APPLE SNACK CAKE
Fourth! Mr. Nussbaum was her fourth husband. Pancho was number three.

PAGE 69: HOLIDAY CIDER PUNCH
Milwaukee is about eighty miles north of Chicago and during the Prohibition Era was under the influence and sometimes protection of Al Capone.

PAGE 71: "SPIKED" ORANGE EGGNOG
Tom & Jerry! The drink was created in England in 1820 and is drunk hot. The cartoon duo debuted in 1940.

PAGE 72: "SUGAR LIPS" SMOOTHIE
Two! Howard Cunningham has his removed in season one and Fonzie has his removed in season five. (Joanie and Richie have already had theirs removed.)

PAGE 74: HOT CHOCOLATE WITH TINY MARSHMALLOWS
Officer Kirk was always convinced that Fonzie was the mastermind of nearly every crime in town.

PAGE 79: ARNOLD'S CHERRY LIMEADE
It's never fully explained, but Richie mentions that he heard Paula joined a convent and became a nun at Arnold's wedding at the end of season three.

PAGE 80: K.C.'S STRAWBERRY BASIL ICED TEA
K.C.'s boarding school in Houston unexpectedly and suddenly closed when the headmaster of the junior class was found with pictures, lots of pictures. Of what? We don't know!

PAGE 88: FOOD FIGHT ROLLS WITH HERB BUTTER
Ron's brother, Clint Howard, appears in season eight as Junior Leopard Donald Jr., son of prankster Lodge member, Donald Hedges.

PAGE 89: CRANBERRY SAUCE
They were busy watching the big football game on television. (The Green Bay Packers won.)

PAGE 91: FRESH-BUTTERED SWEET PEAS
They receive a dead fish (Joanie's joke) and a weekend cabin rental at Lake Whitefish.

PAGE 93: GREEN BEANS ALMONDINE
Marion majored in archaeology!

PAGE 94: MUSHROOM WILD RICE
A broken pocket watch—it's as unreliable as Vito was.

PAGE 98: EVEN RALPH CAN MAKE THEM SMASHED POTATOES
Laverne & Shirley (1976–'83), *Blansky's Beauties* (1977), *Mork & Mindy* (1978–'82), *Out of the Blue* (1979), *Joanie Loves Chachi* (1982–'83).

PAGE 99: DUDE RANCH BAKED BARBEQUE BEANS
Trick question! Uncle Ben never appears on screen during the three episodes of "Westward Ho!" in season six.

PAGE 101: LEOPARD LODGE OVEN-ROASTED CORN ON THE COB
Fraternal Order of the Bass: Their fez was dark blue emblazoned with a silver sequin cursive "B."

PAGE 102: PIZZA BOWL AIR-FRIED MOZZARELLA STICKS
Not exactly—inspiration for the Pizza Bowl was the Falcon Bowl, in the then Polish-Italian neighborhood Riverwest, which is a short drive or long walk from *Happy Days* creator Thomas Miller's teenage home in the Milwaukee suburb of Shorewood. The Falcon Bowl was built in 1898 and is one of the oldest bowling alleys in the United States.

PAGE 105: FRENCH FRIES
It's Tony Randall doing a funny, over-the-top scene of melodramatic romance.

PAGE 106: ONION RINGS
Ricky Nelson burgers—while onion rings were always available, the Ricky Nelson burger never made it on the menu board.

PAGE 111: MRS. C.'S MEATLOAF
The catchphrase no longer reflected the growth of Fonzie's character. As Fonzie tells Richie in the "Welcome Home" episode of the final season, "I haven't said 'a-mundo' in an awful long time!"

PAGE 115: "CURE-ALL" CHICKEN SOUP WITH DUMPLINGS
He tries to sneak him pizza.

PAGE 119: TV DINNER SALISBURY STEAK
Joanie attended college to earn her teaching degree.

PAGE 120: SUNDAY BAKED HAM
Their favorite team is the Green Bay Packers. The Packers are the only NFL team in Wisconsin and have inspired fan loyalty since their founding in 1919.

PAGE 123: WINE-SOAKED ROAST TURKEY AND GRAVY
His name was Twinkletoes Peters.

PAGE 127: CITY CHICKEN (MOCK CHICKEN LEGS)
Billie Bird played Mother Kelp, a veteran film and television actress who was one of the handful of women named as an honorary Green Beret in recognition for her work entertaining troops in Vietnam.

PAGE 131: CHACHI'S MOM'S SPAGHETTI AND MEATBALLS IN RED SAUCE
John Travolta's mom, Ellen Travolta, played Chachi's mom.

PAGE 133: OVEN-BROASTED CHICKEN
Avalon performs his 1959 number-one hit, "Venus."

PAGE 136: AL'S FISH FRY WITH TARTAR SAUCE
Al Molinaro! Who better to portray your twin brother than you.

PAGE 140: CHICKEN CORDON BLEU à LA CHEZ ANTOINE
Dinner for two cost $38.

PAGE 147: MRS. PICCALO'S CANDY APPLE FLUFF
Four times! Fonzie has appeared as the "Widow Fonzarelli," the super nerd Artie, the front half of a cow, and in a nightie and head cap while trapped in the women's dormitory with Richie.

PAGE 148: ANYTIME PUMPKIN PIE
Sabu was his secret name, a reference to the single-named actor Sabu who rose to fame during the 1930s for his work in adventure films.

PAGE 151: JUNIOR CHIPMUNK'S POKE CAKE
The Lone Ranger! Fonzie can't talk when Howard makes his dreams come true and arranges for the Masked Man to come to Arnold's to wish Fonz a happy birthday.

PAGE 152: BLUEBERRY SHORTCAKE
Richie is allergic to strawberries!

PAGE 155: PATTON VOCATIONAL HIGH SCHOOL CAFETERIA SLAB CHEESECAKE
Crispin Glover—Glover has carved out a career by taking on challenging roles and imbuing them with frantic energy or quiet menace.

PAGE 159: HA-CHA-CHA BROWNIES
He's an optometrist who saves Fonzie's eyesight in season six.

PAGE 160: "BAG" ZOMBROSKI'S DEMON ZUCCHINI BREAD
No one won. They *all* ran through Arnold's parking lot at midnight, though Bag didn't go willingly and had to be carried by the guys.

PAGE 161: GRANDPA CUNNINGHAM'S IRISH FRUITCAKE
Danny Thomas—Thomas was a producer on *The Andy Griffith Show* and had known Ron Howard since he was a wee Opie.

PAGE 163: MORK'S RED, WHITE, AND BLUE GELATIN
Laverne DeFazio—the date does not go well.

PAGE 165: ARNOLD'S WORLD-FAMOUS FROZEN SOFT-SERVE CUSTARD
Anson Williams is a successful director.

ABOUT THE AUTHOR

As a Milwaukee native and longtime fan, I've had so much fun reliving childhood memories of *Happy Days*. My record for catching quarters off my elbow is twelve. I had a cute black stripey cat named Chachi. I owned a copy of *Fonzie Favorites* record. I even skipped out of school in 1983 to meet the cast of *Happy Days* at the airport during a promotional tour. But what I remember best is watching the show with my dad and siblings, laughing at the corny jokes, and feeling like we would have fit in just fine at Arnold's.

You may have seen me riding around Milwaukee with Padma Lakshmi in the Wienermobile on "Taste the Nation." When not writing recipes and watching old episodes of *Happy Days*, I write about the history of food in the United States (*Holy Food: How Cults, Communes, and Religious Movements Influenced What We Eat—An American History*, 2023 and *American Advertising Cookbooks: How Corporations Taught Us to Love Spam®, Bananas, and Jell-O*, 2019). In addition to that, I am the Master Food Preserver for Milwaukee County and the Vice President/Editor of an independent publishing company. You can find more of my work at www.christinaward.net.

Dedication

For everyone who yelled, "Sit on it!" and anyone who longed for a motorcycle and a leather jacket like Fonzie's.

ACKNOWLEDGMENTS

Thank you to the Milky Way Drive-In (1943–1977), the inspiration for Arnold's, and Leon's Frozen Custard (1942–present day), where my father-in-law worked as a teenager in the '40s and still makes the best Butter Pecan Frozen Custard in the universe. Thank you also to my dad who taught me how to ride a motorcycle like Fonzie when I was nine years old!

DIETARY RESTRICTIONS

V = Vegetarian, V+ = Vegan, GF = Gluten-Free

Dude Ranch Breakfast Skillet **GF**

Blueberry Hill Pancakes **V**

Joanie's French Toast **V**

Cunningham's Strengthening Scottish Oatmeal

    Sweet Style **V, GF**

    Savory Styles **GF**

"Morning, Mrs. C.!" Granola **V, GF**

Mr. C.'s Weekend Hash with Poached Eggs **GF**

Pork Sausage Apple Roulade Roast

Leopard Lodge Potato Salad

    Howard's German Style

    Marion's American Style **V, GF**

Cunningham Coleslaw **V, GF**

Wedge Salad **GF**

Pfister Salad **V, GF**

Homemade Honey-Cinnamon Peanut Butter and Raspberry Jam Sandwich **V**

    Honey-Cinnamon Peanut Butter **V, GF**

    Quick Raspberry Jam **V, V+, GF**

Richie's Favorite Sardine Sandwich

Hawaiian Lū'au Club Sandwich with Secret Sandwich Spread

"From the Store" Sandwich Bread **V, V+**

    Whole-Wheat Variation **V**

    Rye Variation **V**

The Bopper and Big Bopper Burgers

Fonzie's Favorite Fried Onions **V, GF**

Hot Diggity Dog and Daddy-O Dog

Arnold's Slow Cooker Chili

Momo Burger

The Big "A" Sloppy Joe Sandwich

Delux B.L.T.

Splish-Splash Tuna Melt Sandwich

Grilled Cheese with Peanuts **V**

Fonzie's Mom's Cinnamon Shortbread Cookies **V**

Malachi Crunch Spicy Snack Mix

Jump the Shark Candy Sushi

Fig Bar Cookies **V**

Potato Chip Cookies **V**

Apple Snack Cake **V**

Old-Fashioned Chocolate Chip Cookies **V**

Rugelach **V**

Holiday Cider Punch **V, GF**

"Spiked" Orange Eggnog **V, GF**

"Sugar Lips" Smoothie **V, GF**

Hot Chocolate with Tiny Marshmallows **V, GF**

Potsie's "Ketchup" Freeze **V, V+, GF**

Arnold's Cherry Limeade **V, V+, GF**

K.C.'s Strawberry Basil Iced Tea **V, GF**

Curried Pan-Fried Carrots **V, GF**

Mr. C.'s "Feed the Platoon" Candied Yams **V, GF**

Food Fight Rolls with Herb Butter **V**

Cranberry Sauce **V, V+, GF**

Kelp Family Chestnut Stuffing **V**

Fresh-Buttered Sweet Peas **GF**

Green Beans Almondine **V, GF**

Mushroom Wild Rice **V, GF**

Joanie's Baked Macaroni and Cheese **V**

Even Ralph Can Make Them Smashed Potatoes **V, GF**

Dude Ranch Baked Barbeque Beans

Leopard Lodge Oven-Roasted Corn on the Cob **V, GF**

Pizza Bowl Air-Fried Mozzarella Sticks **V**

French Fries **V, V+, GF**

Onion Rings **V**

Slow-Roasted Brisket

Mrs. C.'s Meatloaf

Mr. C.'s Favorite Pot Roast

"Cure-All" Chicken Soup with Dumplings

Joanie's Favorite Pork Chops and Applesauce

    Pork Chops **GF**

    Applesauce **V, V+, GF**

TV Dinner Salisbury Steak

Sunday Baked Ham **GF**

Wine-Soaked Roast Turkey and Gravy

City Chicken (Mock Chicken Legs)

"Swedish" Meatballs

Chachi's Mom's Spaghetti and Meatballs in Red Sauce

    Red Sauce **V, V+, GF**

    Meatballs

    Fresh Pasta **V**

Oven-Broasted Chicken

Arnold's Air-Fried Chicken Stand Tenders

Al's Fish Fry with Tartar Sauce

Pizza Bowl Sheet Pan Pizza

Chicken Cordon Bleu à la Chez Antoine

Shrimp-and-Crab Stuffed Crepes à la Chez Antoine

Oysters Rockefeller à la Chez Antoine

Mrs. Piccalo's Candy Apple Fluff **V, GF**

Anytime Pumpkin Pie **V**

Chocolate Layer Cake **V**

Junior Chipmunk's Poke Cake **V**

Blueberry Shortcake **V**

Patton Vocational High School Cafeteria Slab Cheesecake **V**

Ralph Malph's Cherries Jubilee **V, GF**

Ha-Cha-Cha Brownies **V**

"Bag" Zombroski's Demon Zucchini Bread **V**

Grandpa Cunningham's Irish Fruitcake **V**

Mork's Red, White, and Blue Gelatin

Arnold's World-Famous Frozen Soft-Serve Custard **V, GF**

Thick Milwaukee Malt **V**

Banana Boat **V, GF**

Cra-a-zy Crunch Sundae **V**

    Arnold's Toffee Crunch **V, GF**

    Strawberry Crunch **V**

INSIGHT
EDITIONS

PO Box 3088
San Rafael, CA 94912
www.insighteditions.com

 Find us on Facebook: www.facebook.com/InsightEditions
 Follow us on Instagram: @insighteditions

ISBN: 979-8-88663-356-6

Publisher: Raoul Goff
VP, Co-Publisher: Vanessa Lopez
VP, Creative: Chrissy Kwasnik
VP, Manufacturing: Alix Nicholaeff
Publishing Director: Jamie Thompson
Art Director: Stuart Smith
Designer: Leah Bloise Lauer
Editor: Sami Alvarado
VP, Executive Project Editor: Vicki Jaeger
Production Associate: Deena Hashem
Senior Production Manager, Subsidiary Rights: Lina s Palma-Temena

Photography by Waterbury Publications, Inc.

Insight Editions, in association with Roots of Peace, will plant two trees for each tree used in the manufacturing of this book. Roots of Peace is an internationally renowned humanitarian organization dedicated to eradicating land mines worldwide and converting war-torn lands into productive farms and wildlife habitats. Roots of Peace will plant two million fruit and nut trees in Afghanistan and provide farmers there with the skills and support necessary for sustainable land use.

Manufactured in China by Insight Editions

10 9 8 7 6 5 4 3 2 1

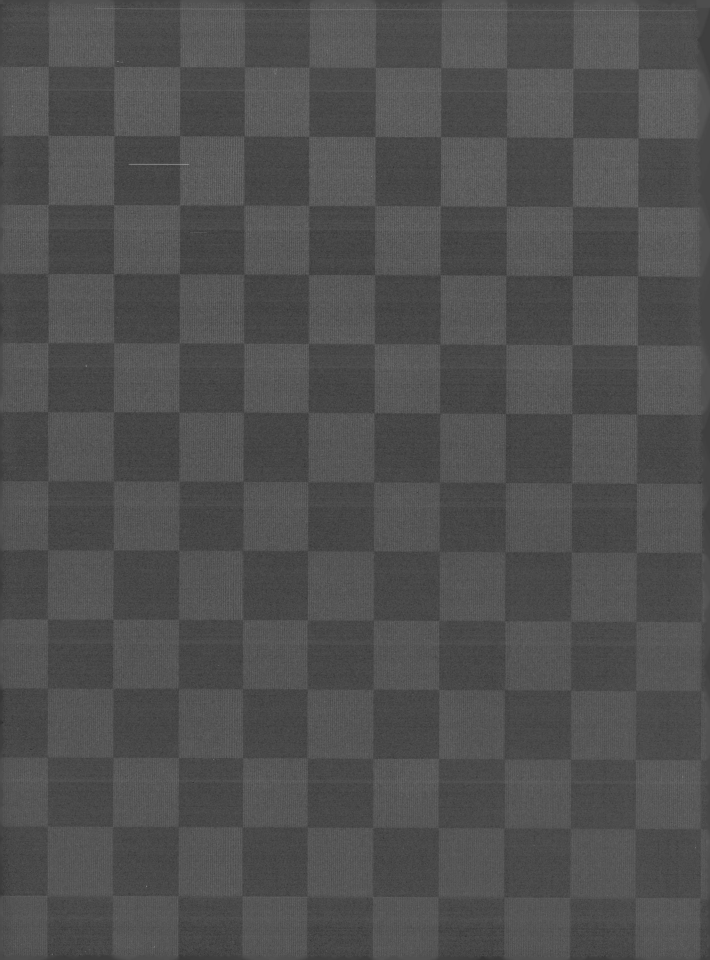